*T*his book
belongs to

_____

...*a woman after God's
own heart.*

Nurturing a Heart of Humility

Elizabeth George

HARVEST HOUSE™ PUBLISHERS

EUGENE, OREGON

Cover by Terry Dugan Design, Bloomington, Minnesota

Acknowledgments

As always, thank you to my dear husband, Jim George, M.Div., Th.M., for your able assistance, guidance, suggestions, and loving encouragement on this project.

NURTURING A HEART OF HUMILITY
Copyright © 2002 Elizabeth George
Published by Harvest House Publishers
Eugene, Oregon 97402
www.harvesthousepublishers.com

ISBN–13: 978-0-7369-0300-4
ISBN–10: 0-7369-0300-3

Contents

Foreword

For some time I have been looking for Bible studies that I could use each day that would increase my knowledge of God's Word. In my search, I found myself struggling between two extremes: Bible studies that required little time but also had little substance, or studies that were in-depth and demanded more time than I could give. I discovered that I wasn't alone—there were many other women like me who were busy yet desired to spend quality time studying God's Word.

That's why I became excited when Elizabeth George shared her desire to create a series of women's Bible studies that offered in-depth lessons that could be completed in just 15-20 minutes per day. When she completed the first study—on Philippians—I was eager to try it out. I had already studied Philippians many times, but this was the first time I had come to understand exactly how the whole book fit together and how it can truly be lived out in my life. Each lesson was simple but insightful—and was written especially to apply to me as a woman!

In the Woman After God's Own Heart® Bible study series, Elizabeth takes you step by step through the Scriptures, sharing wisdom she has gleaned from more than 20 years as a women's Bible teacher. The lessons are rich and meaningful because they're rooted in God's Word and have been lived out in Elizabeth's life. Her thoughtful and personable guidance make you feel as though you are studying right alongside her—as if she is personally mentoring you in the greatest aspiration you could ever pursue: to become a woman after God's own heart.

If you're looking for Bible studies that can help you grow stronger in your knowledge of God's Word even in the most demanding of schedules, I know you'll find this series to be a welcome companion in your daily walk with God.

—LaRae Weikert
Editorial Managing Director,
Harvest House Publishers

Before You Begin

In my book *A Woman After God's Own Heart,*® I describe such a woman as one who ensures that God is first in her heart and the Ultimate Priority of her life. Then I share that one crucial way this desire can become reality is by nurturing a heart that abides in God's Word. To do so means that you and I must develop a root system anchored deep in God's Word.

Before you launch into this Bible study, take a moment to think about these aspects of a root system produced by the regular, faithful study of God's Word:

- *Roots are unseen*—You'll want to set aside time in solitude— "underground" if you will—to immerse yourself in God's Word and grow in Him.

- *Roots are for taking in*—Alone and with your Bible in hand, you'll want to take in and feed upon the truths of the Word of God and ensure your spiritual growth.

- *Roots are for storage*—As you form the habit of looking into God's Word, you'll find a vast, deep reservoir of divine hope and strength forming for the rough times.

- *Roots are for support*—Do you want to stand strong in the Lord? To stand firm against the pressures of life? The routine care of your roots through exposure to God's Word will cultivate you into a remarkable woman of endurance.[1]

I'm glad you've chosen this study out of my A Woman After God's Own Heart® Bible study series. My prayer for you is that the truths you find in God's Word through this study will further transform your life into the image of His dear Son and empower you to be the woman you seek to be: a woman after God's own heart.

In His love,

Elizabeth George

Lesson 1

Finishing the Masterpiece

inishing?! As you look at this title and consider that this lesson is actually the *beginning* of our study of the lovely life of Mary, the mother of our Lord, are you wondering why we're starting this way?

As we'll discover, every finished masterpiece, including God's great Masterpiece, is painted in stages. I well remember a privileged visit to the home and studio of artist Sandy Lynam Clough. Sandy has a special place in my heart because one of her paintings graces the cover of my book *Loving God with All Your Mind*.[2] In fact, her cover painting is so expressive that women regularly tell me that it makes them want to curl up in a chair, drink a cup of tea, and read their Bible...just like the picture on the book invites!

Well, as I was busy snapping photographs of Sandy's work studio, I noticed a painting on her easel that was only partially done. The sketch and composition were obvious but the details were missing. Her painting's images were cloudy and vague, lacking the clarity soon to be inserted by their master's hand.

And, my dear studying friend, as we begin considering the events of the four Gospels of the New Testament and of the life of Mary, we see distant images "painted" by Old Testament prophets come into sharper focus. As we step up to inspect those events yet to come, we sense that God's masterpiece—the one He began to reveal in the chapters and books of the Old Testament—is yet to be finished. We ponder seemingly unfulfilled purposes, promises, and prophecies.

As we look at the New Testament gospels and the story they tell, however, we begin to understand God's purposes as prophecies are indeed fulfilled through the life of Mary's Son. By the time our study is finished, we will see God's masterpiece of the promised Messiah finished and unveiled! And we'll also see how a humble Jewish girl's life was masterfully painted onto the canvas of these New Testament accounts.

From the Heart of God's Word...

1. Where does the record of the life of Mary begin? And where is the best place to begin our study? Read Isaiah 7:14 and copy it here.

Now read how Matthew interprets this Old Testament passage in Matthew 1:21-23. Make your notes here.

2. Look up Micah 5:2 and copy it here.

   This is another prophecy about the birth of Jesus Christ—He would be the "ruler in Israel" and would be born in Bethlehem (Luke 2:4-7).

3. Next read Luke 3:23-38. Don't let this genealogy of Mary's lineage overwhelm you. Begin by listing the names you are already familiar with.

It's important to understand that the genealogy in Luke 3 gives the *human* line of Jesus, the son of man, tracing His lineage through Mary (Heli in verse 23 was Mary's father) back to Adam. First-century people thought Jesus was the son of Joseph. Luke made it clear that Jesus was actually *God's* Son and that Mary was His mother.

From Your Heart...

As we step into our study, realize that 400 years have passed since the conclusion of Malachi, the last book of the Old Testament. And in the biblical record, over 500 years have gone by without a miracle. Bible scholars call these years "the silent years." What happens when God is silent...or *seems* to be silent? How did God's people behave during those silent years? And what did they believe?

The people you'll be meeting in the scriptures below (and in the days and lessons to follow) show us the answers to these questions—they served God...period. They were not wanting something more. True, they looked with anticipation for the promised Messiah. But they woke up each and every day of their lives and sought to live a righteous life before God. They endeavored to trust and obey, to walk and yield to God's already-expressed will.

Now, how are *you* to live while waiting upon God to finish His masterpiece and His master plan for your life?

- *Live expectantly*—God's people during any age are to live with the anticipation of God's redemption. What was Simeon in Luke 2:25-26 expecting?

  And Anna in Luke 2:38?

  And, as a bonus question, *how* did these saints live while waiting?

  —Simeon (Luke 2:25)?

  —Anna (Luke 2:37)?

- *Live in obedience*—How did Elizabeth and Zacharias in Luke 1:6 conduct their daily lives while living expectantly?

  And Mary in Luke 1:30 and 38?

  And Joseph in Matthew 1:19?

  How well do you measure up in your own obedience as compared to...Simeon?

...Anna?

...Elizabeth and Zacharias?

...Mary and Joseph?

* *Live with understanding*—God is *never* silent, and He is *always* at work directing the course of events throughout the world to bring about His perfect will in His perfect time. He rules the changing tides of history. How does Psalm 75:6-7 comfort you and encourage you to live— and wait!—with understanding?

Nurturing a Heart of Humility

Dear one, we must also *live humbly.* This is a study about Mary, a woman after God's own heart, a woman desirous of fulfilling God's will for her life (Acts 13:23). And the lessons to come will reveal that Mary was a woman with a heart of humility. So, how do you and I set about to nurture the same heart of humility toward God and others that we'll find Mary exhibiting throughout these pages?

Read your Bible regularly—The Bible discloses God's will for your life. Once you know what His will is, then you can humbly obey it.

Pray regularly. Prayer develops a heart—and a posture— of humility. Prayer also helps to bring your will in line with God's will.

Worship regularly—God asks for your worship—both private and corporate worship. When you worship you are submitting yourself to be quiet before God and to be taught by Him and by others. Both acts nurture humility in your heart.

Serve others regularly—Whom should you serve? Serve your family first...and beyond them, serve anyone and everyone who crosses your path. Service is the outworking of humility.

And now, may God richly bless *you* as you nurture a heart of humility, for "humility is the Christian's loveliest virtue and his crowning grace."[3]

Living in Humility

Luke 1:5-25

*W*hat's in a name? Well, for starters, consider the name of the wonderful woman after God's own heart you'll be meeting in this lesson—Elizabeth...which just happens to be my name too! I carry in my personal leatherbound journal a tasseled, laminated, tapestry bookmark that was given to me by a cherished friend. It reads *Elizabeth—Consecrated to God*. Two scriptures are also woven into the ribbon: "My soul doth magnify the Lord" (Luke 1:46 KJV) and "A good name is rather to be chosen than great riches" (Proverbs 22:1 KJV).

Elizabeth means "God is my oath" and "a worshiper of God."[4] And today we meet a woman who lived out the meanings of her name. This humble woman was chosen by God to play a most important role in His final countdown to the Savior's appearance.

15

From the Heart of God's Word...

As you work your way through these verses from Luke 1, keep three things in mind—*first,* a theme of Luke's Gospel is that nothing is impossible with God (Luke 1:37); *second,* God's will is always perfect; and *third,* so is His timing (Luke 1:20)!

1. Luke 1:5-7—Who is the couple introduced in verse 5, and what is said about each?

   —

   —

   How is this godly couple described in verse 6?

   What distressing news is added in verse 7?

2. Luke 1:8-22—As we key in on Zacharias, what miracle occurred in his life in verse 11?

   And what information and instruction was Zacharias given (verse 13)?

   Briefly, how is the child-to-be described (verses 14-17)?

What question of unbelief did Zacharias ask...and how did the angel reply (verses 18-20)?

What happened when Zacharias came out of the temple (verses 21-22)?

3. Luke 1:23-25—In the end, what happened to...

...Zacharias?

...Elizabeth?

From Your Heart...

* *Character*—Barrenness apparently carried a reproach in the culture of this couple's day (Luke 1:25). In spite of their personal difficulty and sorrow, how is the character of this godly couple described (verse 6)?

How do you, dear reader, tend to cope with difficulty, discouragement, and disappointment? How consistent are you in your devotion to God during times of adversity? And how does Elizabeth and Zacharias's steadfast devotion over decades of blighted hopes show you a better way?

- *Consecrated*—As we learned earlier, *Elizabeth* means "consecrated," and *consecrated* means "set apart unto God." What did the angel Gabriel say about the son Elizabeth was to bear (verse 15)?

This is a reference to a *Nazirite vow*—John was to be a Nazirite, a person separated completely and consecrated unto the Lord (Numbers 6:2-8).

Just for fun, note the names of these famous sons who were also Nazirites, consecrated to the Lord from the womb:

> Manoah's wife's son in Judges 13:7-24—
>
> Hannah's son in 1 Samuel 1:11,20—

Now copy 1 Peter 1:15-16 here.

Do you see yourself as consecrated to God? As dedicated to Him for His purposes? As separated from the world for God's use? As a believer, you are, whether you see it or not! What difference should this fact make in your daily life?

- *Chastised*—There's no doubt that Zacharias was chastised by Gabriel for his unbelief! What was the consequence of his unbelief (verse 20)?

Imagine! The most exciting thing in your life has just happened...and you can't tell a soul! What similar temptations to unbelief do you face? And how should you be responding with greater faith?

* *Conception*—How did Elizabeth respond to her conception (verse 24)? And what did she say in her heart (verse 25)?

Nurturing a Heart of Humility

Life is difficult—it's a fact! And "God asks no man whether he will accept life. That is not the choice. You *must* take it. The only choice is *how*."[5] Elizabeth and Zacharias show us the *how*—the proper, godly, humble response to discouragement, disappointment, and blighted dreams. What can we learn from them? We must...

* Nurture a heart of prayer (Luke 1:13).
* Nurture a heart of obedience (Luke 1:6).
* Nurture a heart of service (Luke 1:8).
* Nurture a heart of humility.

Elizabeth was finally given a child—in God's timing and for God's purposes...and in a miraculous way! And when God blessed her, hers was a humble response. She acknowledged and blessed the Lord. Elizabeth gave thanks and recognition and glory to God.

But what if Elizabeth and her husband had never received the child they prayed for and hoped for? They would prob- ably have continued to be the same couple they had always been and had become—a couple whose hearts were humbly set on prayer, obedience, and service.

Could the same be said of you, dear one?

esson 3

Finding Favor with God

Luke 1:26-33

he kernel of true humility is faith...is trusting in God.

Today we're going to meet a very special young woman who found favor with God and who has a lot to teach us about humility's kernel...about faith. Her name is Mary. And I think by the time you've finished this lesson you'll realize that, when it comes to faith and favor with God,

>...they have nothing to do with age—Mary was only a young teenage woman.

>...they have nothing to do with wealth or position—Mary had neither.

>...they have nothing to do with gender—Mary was a woman, which, in her day, made her next-to-unusable.

No, faith and favor with God have nothing to do with externals. But they have everything to do with how we *respond* to the externals. We don't know for certain the details of how Mary's faith was formed, but we do see how it performed...and found favor with God. Let's look now at this young woman after God's own heart, this girl of great faith.

From the Heart of God's Word...

1. In our previous lesson, we met Elizabeth, who is now miraculously pregnant with John the Baptist. In this lesson the same angel, Gabriel, visits the cousin of Elizabeth. Give the details of that visit found in Luke 1:26-27:

   Who is present in this scene?

   How is Mary described?

   When did this visit occur?

   And where did this visit occur?

2. How did Mary respond to the angel Gabriel (verse 29)?

3. How did Gabriel describe the work of her future son (verses 32-33)?

   And what was His name to be (verse 31)?

From Your Heart...

• Twice, the angel Gabriel spoke to Mary about her standing with God. What did he say in...

...verse 28—

...verse 30—

What is it, according to Hebrews 11:6, that causes people to please God and find His favor? Copy the entire verse here.

• Bible scholars teach us that a young woman was usually betrothed or engaged at about age twelve or twelve-and-a-half.[6] Therefore, Mary was most likely in her early teens as we meet her in Luke 1. And yet Mary's faith in God was well formed by such a tender age.

If you are a mother, what are you doing to help cultivate the faith of your daughters and sons? By age 12 to 14, Mary had already learned to trust in God and in His Word. Could the same be said for your children? Why or why not?

What insight does 2 Timothy 3:15 give you as a parent seeking to nurture a heart of faith in your children?

- And, what are you doing to cultivate *your* faith? How is *your* faith quotient when it comes to trusting in God and in His Word? Take a few minutes to glance back at the issues of the past week. How did you exhibit great faith...or not-so-great faith?

What do these scriptures teach us about faith?

Romans 10:17—

Hebrews 11:1—

How will you begin to strengthen your faith this week?

Nurturing a Heart of Humility

Mary exhibits the kind of faith you and I, as women after God's own heart, must nurture in ourselves and in our children. She shows us how God can use any woman, regardless of age and status, if that woman will love Him, obey Him, and trust in Him.

Many women erroneously think that they're not anyone special, that they are deficient in areas that the world deems essential, that they need more education, better clothes, a better resume, a better pedigree—the list goes on. But, my dear friend, as Mary's humble life teaches us, if you love God—if you seek after Him with all your heart and if you obey Him because you love Him—you, like Mary, will enjoy His favor.

Do you want to do extraordinary things for God? Then start by simply loving and obeying Him. Mary's love for God qualified her to be used by God. She was poor, young, and unknown, but she exhibited a faith that was pleasing in God's sight. Therefore she found favor with Him.

esson 4

Submitting from the Heart

Luke 1:34-38

What has happened to true humility?! Why is it so rare? Hear these words from the pen of another:

> A spirit of humility is very rare in our day of strong-willed, proud-as-a-peacock attitudes. The clenched fist has replaced the bowed head. The big mouth and the surly stare now dominate the scene once occupied by the quiet godliness of the "poor in spirit."[7]

These are sobering words, aren't they? And frightening, too! However, in Mary we find an example of true humility. Let's learn from her now about nurturing a heart of humility.

From the Heart of God's Word...

1. Read again Luke 1:26-33. What one question did Mary ask the angel Gabriel about the events that were to come, and why (verse 34)?

How did Mary's question in verse 34 differ from that of Zacharias (see verses 18-20)?

2. What words did the angel use to describe the conception of Mary's baby (verse 35)?

And how did he describe the baby (verse 35)?

3. What other miraculous information did Gabriel share with Mary (verse 36)?

And what was Gabriel's final statement to Mary (verse 37)?

4. In the end, how did Mary indicate a heart of humility in her answer to Gabriel (verse 38)?

Also, how did Mary refer to herself?

From Your Heart...

- *Situation*—As we compare Zacharias's "how" question (verse 18) with Mary's "how" question (verse 34), it becomes obvious that Mary believed in the promise but didn't understand the performance. Zacharias, however, did not even believe the promise. Instead he asked for a sign.

Can you think of a time when you received shocking and perplexing news, news that announced the further unfolding of God's will for your life? How did you handle it, and how does Mary's faith in God show you a better way for humbly submitting to God's will?

- *Statement*—Record again Mary's statement of self-description in verse 38.

Here Mary describes herself as *doule*, as "a slave girl." Complete obedience marked out a *doule*, one who could not but do the will of her master. Can you say the same of yourself? Or, put another way, is there any reason you cannot say the same of yourself in your relationship with your Master, the Lord Jesus Christ? Is there any area of hold-out in your obedience? And, if so, what will you do about it today? This week?

- *Submission*—Copy Mary's famous statement of utter submission to the will of God for her life found in verse 38.

So often we struggle with God and postpone our submission. And even in Mary's case, a rash of human emotions and responses probably raced through her mind. And with good reason!

> Wonder—Mary didn't understand (verse 34).
>
> Fear—Mary was troubled (verses 29-30).
>
> Distress—Mary probably knew the penalty for pregnancy outside marriage was death by stoning (Leviticus 20:10).
>
> Troubled—How could she explain this to others? To Joseph, her spouse-to-be?
>
> Questioning—Mary was a virgin and unmarried. *How* could/would this happen?

But, in the end, in quiet heroism, this girl of great faith, this slave, this maidservant of the Lord, submitted willingly and humbly—and without all the answers!—to God's mysterious will for her life.

Now let's do a heart check. How willingly are you submitting to God's will for your life? For sure this is usually a process and a processing! But, in the end, can you say to God, "Anything, anywhere, anytime, at any cost"? If not, why not? Be honest!

Nurturing a Heart of Humility

Beloved, Mary's submission was from the heart. Hers was a humble heart—the humble heart of a *doule*—and a heart of pure faith. In essence her heart reply to God was, "I live to serve You. I desire no life apart from You. I will do whatever You ask because I belong to You. I will do whatever You ask, quietly and without question. Let it be to me according to Your word."

Now, can you—in quiet godliness, with bowed head and heart, as one poor in spirit—say along with the young Mary, "Let it be to me according to Your word"?

Lesson 5

Encouraging Others

Luke 1:39-45

You will love this completely positive scene that we encounter today in our study of the life of Mary! It is utterly uplifting!

Every woman's life is visited by problems, difficulties, challenges. We're busy. We're burdened. And we carry the burdens of our loved ones in our hearts as well. In Elizabeth and Mary we meet two such women. Neither of them had—or would have—an easy life. Elizabeth had lived decades of heartache. And Mary's decades of heartache were just around the corner.

But in the midst of Elizabeth and Mary's daily woes and the cares of everyday life, we witness this brilliant encounter, this scene filled with the "Holy Spirit," with marvel, with mutual blessing and honor and rejoicing, and with encouragement—as two humble women "do lunch," so to speak.

Read on to discover the ministry that can occur whenever two of God's women get together.

From the Heart of God's Word...

1. Read again Luke 1:24-25 to review the details of Elizabeth's situation. Summarize these details in one sentence.

   Then read again Luke 1:34-38 to review the details of Mary's situation. Summarize these details in one sentence.

2. Now read Luke 1:39-45 and note these facts:

   Where does this scene take place?

   When does this scene take place?

   Who is present and what do we know about them (verse 36)?

3. What happened to Elizabeth when the pregnant Mary came into her house (verses 41 and 44)?

   How did Elizabeth greet Mary (verse 42)?

   And how did Elizabeth refer to Mary (verse 43)?

Blessing upon blessing! How did Elizabeth continue to "bless" Mary in verse 45?

From Your Heart...

• *Elizabeth*—In Elizabeth we find a Bible portrait of a woman of character. The Bible reports that Elizabeth...

✓ was filled with the Holy Spirit, who enabled her as she
✓ spoke forth remarkable praise and
✓ affirmed and ministered to young Mary

Now, make your own list of the many indications of Elizabeth's humility. For instance, where is her focus? Who is she speaking of?

How can you follow in Elizabeth's footsteps in your relationships with other Christian women?

I can't help but interject these thoughts here: These are the first words we hear Elizabeth speak (other than those probably spoken to herself in her heart in verse 25). A miracle had occurred in the life and body of each woman. And Elizabeth was perhaps as much as 40 to 50 years older than her young relative, Mary. Yet Elizabeth had no problem in seeing Mary's joy as greater than her own. She had no problem honoring and blessing Mary. She had no problem humbling herself before Mary as "the mother of her Lord."

The world has yet to see what could happen if everyone lost the desire to get the glory. Wouldn't it be a marvelous place if no one cared who got the credit?[8]

* *Encounter*—Quickly scan verses 46-56. Both of these women are indeed humble! As we'll see in our next few lessons, they bless one another as they worship God together and exult in God's work. This is a true interchange of the "good things" of the Lord (Titus 2:3) being shared between an older woman and a younger woman. Their encounter is truly one of mutual blessing and encouragement!

Read now Titus 2:3-5. As you seek to grow in the Lord, what qualities should you aspire to according to verses 3-4a?

And how do you see these qualities listed for the "older women" lived out in Elizabeth as she ministers to Mary?

* *Ending*—Because our study is about Mary and her Son, we are saying farewell to this noble, older saint, Elizabeth. But you need to know how her story ended. You need to know two things:

—Her special little boy baby was born (please read verses 57-80—it was quite an event!), and...

—He grew to become the forerunner of the Messiah, Jesus Christ (please read verses 13-17 and verses 76-77). We speak of Elizabeth's son today as "John the Baptist" (Matthew 3:1).

Elizabeth's life was one of humble usefulness to God. What do these scriptures teach us about humility?

Matthew 23:12—

1 Peter 5:5—

1 Peter 5:6—

Now read Luke 1:6. How do you see these truths about humility illustrated by Elizabeth's life?

Nurturing a Heart of Humility

Beloved, what do you tend to talk about when you are with other Christian women? We have so many options, don't we? We can choose to talk about trivia, trash, the latest "talk" from a talk show, the local news, gossip, or—our most well-loved topic—ourself!

If we are nurturing a heart of humility, our "talk" will be markedly different! Why? Because as women who are humble—women after God's own heart—we will think of others. We will be other-oriented. We will, like Elizabeth, seek to encourage others, honor others, bless others, build up others. One of the principles of my life I owe to a principle from one of my husband Jim's sermons: *Make it your goal that, in every encounter, others are better off for having been in your presence.*

Dear one, such a goal assists both you and me as we seek to be women who encourage others!

Lesson 6

Magnifying the Lord

Luke 1:46-56

*H*umility is what I call a "fuzzy" virtue. It's desirable. It's admirable. But it's also next-to-undefinable! It's hard to get your hands on exactly what this soft, heavenly, ethereal trait is. Well, dear student of the Word, prepare yourself today to come to grips with the meaning of humility. Prepare yourself to gaze upon a portrait of true humility!

I'm talking about Mary and the picture God paints of her in today's portion of Scripture. You and I can thank God that He has preserved for all time this depiction of humility in His Word. That means that you and I can always revisit it and be refreshed and reminded over and over again about God's high calling upon our lives to nurture a heart of humility.

Perhaps no other woman was as blessed by God as was the lowly Mary (1:28,39,42,45). God chose Mary (a teenager

37

who just happened to be a young woman after His own heart!) to bring His Son into this world. Yet, in spite of her exalted favor and blessing by God, Mary humbly bows her head, her knee, and her heart…to worship the Bestower of the blessings, and to magnify the Lord who faithfully keeps His promises and remembers His people. Let's look in on this scene.

From the Heart of God's Word…

1. Reread Luke 1:39-45. Who did the talking in this scene, and what did she say about Mary? Then enjoy the following thought about humility.

> *I*t is no great thing to be humble when you are brought low; but to be humble when you are praised is a great and rare achievement.[9]

2. Now read Luke 1:46-56. How does Mary begin what is called "Mary's Magnificat" (verse 46)?

3. Look now at the key to Mary's humility in verse 47. *Who* did Mary magnify, and *how* did she refer to Him?

4. *Why* did Mary magnify the Lord (verses 47-49)? Be sure to make a complete list! Leave nothing out! You're in for a treat!

From Your Heart...

Three verses—three blessings! Let's "count" them now!

- *Blessing #1—God saved Mary* (verse 47). Mary clearly recognized that she was, like all of mankind, a sinner who needed to trust the Lord for her eternal salvation. What do these verses teach us about our need for a savior?

  Romans 3:10—

  Romans 3:23—

  In the words of Mary's Son, Jesus Christ, what must we do to be saved (John 11:25-26)? Write these verses out. You should memorize them, too, so you can share them with others.

  Can you, my precious friend, say that you, too, are saved? Please explain why or why not.

- *Blessing #2—God "smiled on" Mary* (verse 48). God "regarded" Mary. He was mindful of her. He looked with special favor upon her. Share several of the many ways God has "smiled" on you and shown favor toward you. Then give abundant thanks like Mary did!

- *Blessing #3—God showered Mary with blessings* (verse
  49). This verse is so expressive of the personal gratitude
  that resides in the heart of a woman whom God has
  saved. Why don't you memorize it, too?

Nurturing a Heart of Humility

As we ponder God's many lessons to our hearts from
these few verses, I want us to leave with these two:

God's Word in your heart—Scholars tell us that Mary's
"Magnificat" contains at least 15 discernable quotes from the
Old Testament. You see, Mary knew God through the books
of Moses, the Psalms, and the writings of the prophets. She
had a deep reverence for the Lord God in her heart because
she knew what He had done in the history of her people.[10]

Jesus said, "Out of the abundance of the heart the mouth
speaks" (Matthew 12:34). And David wrote, "Let the words of
my mouth and the meditation of my heart be acceptable in
Your sight" (Psalm 19:14). What comes from your heart and
mouth, my friend? Are you hiding God's Word in your heart
so that when you open your mouth, the overflow of God's
Word comes gushing forth in praise like Mary's "Magnificat"?

God's Son in your heart—Human pride says, "I don't need
anything or anyone!" But the greatest mark of humility is to
acknowledge, "I need a Savior!"

Are you wondering, "Why do I need a Savior?" Consider
all that Jesus the Christ, the Savior whom God sent, offers
you and me. He...

S ubstitutes His sinless life for our sinful one.
A ssures us of eternal life.
V anquishes Satan's hold on our life.
I nitiates us into the family of God.
O verthrows the power of sin.
R econciles us to a holy God.

Are you saved, dear one? If so, magnify the Lord!

Lesson 7

Learning to Pray

Luke 1:46-56

*H*ave you ever been present when someone opened a gathering in prayer, uttering something like this—"Lord, we want to thank You for who You are and what You've done"? Usually the earnest pray-er stops right there...and never says a word about who God is or what He has done! It's almost as if he or she doesn't know what God has done, can't think of what God has done, or doesn't take the time to say what God has done.

Obviously we have lessons to learn today...lessons from a young teenage woman, probably about a 14-year-old. As you read these humble words of glorious exaltation spoken from the heart of Mary, let her—along with Hannah from the Old Testament—teach you how to pray, how to magnify the Lord. Let these women after God's own heart teach you who God is and what He has done!

From the Heart of God's Word...

Before we look again at Mary's life, I want us to meet another woman after God's own heart, another woman with "a song in her heart," another woman who exhibited a heart of humility. Her name is Hannah. Hannah had a hard life— she shared her husband with another wife who had children while Hannah had none. And, to make matters worse, the other wife provoked Hannah daily and relentlessly.

But Hannah handled her dual crisis in the right way—she took it to God in prayer. The result? She conceived a child. She gave birth to a son. And her son served the Lord all his days.

Now, how does Hannah relate to our study of Mary's life? It's just possible that on her four-day walk to Elizabeth's house in the hill country Mary was musing over Hannah's famous Old Testament prayer.

1. Read 1 Samuel 2:1-10. Now compare the verses below from Mary's "Magnificat" (Luke 1:46-56) with those from Hannah's prayer (1 Samuel 2:1-10).

Luke 1:	1 Samuel 2:
46-47	1
49	2
51	4,9,10
52	8
53	5,7

2. In our previous lesson we noted verses 46-49, Mary's response to *what God did for her.* Quickly summarize the contents of these four verses and then let's look at two more portions of Mary's song of praise.

3. Verses 50-53—*what God does for the downtrodden.* Here Mary's words include all of God's people. Who is it that receives God's mercy and help (verse 50)?

What does God do for the helpless (verse 51)?

And for the humble (verse 52)?

And for the hungry (verse 53)?

4. Verses 54-55—*what God will do for Israel.* What did God promise to Abraham and to Israel in...

...Genesis 12:1-3—

...Genesis 17:19—

...Genesis 22:18—

...Genesis 26:4—

...Genesis 28:14—

...Psalm 98:1-3—

All of these promises point to the Messiah's forthcoming appearance—a promise that was about to become reality!

From Your Heart...

- What does Mary say about the character of God in her "Magnificat"? Beware, your list may (and should) be long!

- What do we learn about Mary's character as revealed in her song?

- What do we learn about nurturing a heart of humility from Mary's example in this passage?

Nurturing a Heart of Humility

Dear one, Mary's "Magnificat" is filled to overflowing with information about God—about who He is *and* what He has done! A heart of humility is a heart that prays. So...if you're looking for help with your prayer life or if you're just learning to pray, take a page out of Mary's book. Use her God-inspired words to magnify the Lord.

Handling Life's Crises

Matthew 1:1-25

*N*o matter how carefully we try to live our lives, we are sure to encounter trials (James 1:2) and tribulation (John 16:33). Unfortunately these twins of adversity are facts of life!

So…how do you tend to handle life's crises? Or perhaps a more realistic question is, how did you handle your last crisis?

As we've been learning, Mary was living in the center of a huge crisis. She was pregnant, which was a public disgrace and punishable by stoning (Leviticus 20:10). She was engaged to a righteous man, who was sure to be hurt and would surely want nothing to do with her. As Mary appears to have silently trusted in God, let's see how God used the man Joseph to act on Mary's behalf. And you and I have a front-row seat as we watch how Joseph handled his crisis and assisted Mary in handling hers.

From the Heart of God's Word...

Read Matthew 1:1-17. Don't let this genealogy of Joseph's lineage overwhelm you. Begin by listing the names you are already familiar with. Keep in mind that Joseph's genealogy gave Jesus the legal right to the throne of David (verse 6).

1. Look specifically at verse 16. Because Jesus Christ was of *divine* origin, because He was the Son of *God*, He could not have a human father. That's why Mary is interjected into Joseph's genealogy—Jesus was born of *her*, although Joseph was her husband.

2. Now, get excited! An angel appeared to Joseph a total of five times! *Five times!* What promise (Luke 1:31-35) became fact in Matthew 1:18?

Also what fact does the Word of God make clear regarding sexual relations between Joseph and Mary (verse 18)?

How is Joseph described in verse 19?

And, rather than make Mary a public spectacle, what did Joseph decide to do instead (verse 19)?

Remember as you read that the engagement period, or the betrothal time, was as binding as marriage. Therefore, to break an engagement (or, as the Bible text states, "to put her away") required a legal divorce (verse 19).

3. But…what happened instead (verse 20)?

List the angel's description of Jesus' conception, life, and ministry (verses 20-23).

4. How did Joseph respond to the angel's instructions (verse 24)?

And, once again, what fact does the Word of God make clear regarding sexual relations between Joseph and Mary (verse 25)?

From Your Heart…

This study is about Mary, a woman after God's own heart. But in Joseph we meet a *man* after God's own heart. His heart is evident in three qualities that mark the way he handled a major life crisis.

- *Righteous*—Joseph was a righteous man, a man who desired to handle the situations and crises of his life in the right way—God's way. As he thought through his situation (and crisis!) regarding Mary's pregnancy, what did

Joseph determine was the right thing to do (verse 19) according to the Old Testament (Deuteronomy 24:1)?

*~ Adversity reveals much
about our spiritual character. ~*

What did Joseph's decision in Matthew 1:19 regarding his betrothal to Mary reveal about his spiritual character?

Recall the last crisis you encountered in your own life. What did your actions reveal about your spiritual character? Did you follow God's Word? Please explain.

Pray now and ask God to help you to become the kind of person who desires to respond righteously to the issues of life.

• *Respectful*—How did Joseph demonstrate respect for...

...the angel's instructions (verses 20-25)?

...the angel's explanation (verses 20-21)?

Mary respectfully followed God's instructions...and so did Joseph. Would you characterize yourself as one who submits to God's instructions from His Word? Mary didn't fully understand what was happening to her, but she submitted to God's will and instructions. And the same was true of Joseph.

• *Responsible*—Although Joseph was "afraid" of possible and probable consequences (verse 20) and may have been hurt and/or upset, he responded immediately(!) to the angel's message and took on the responsibility for Mary and her Son. What can we learn from his courageous and immediate obedience?

Nurturing a Heart of Humility

We can't really know the depth of our character until we see how we react under pressure. What seemed to be a crisis in Mary's life...and Joseph's, too...was God working out His will for this couple. And both passed the test of faith, teaching us all along the way! Both humbly bowed to God's will. Both handled their crisis righteously, respectfully, and responsibly.

Dear one, God has lessons in humility He wants us to learn as we encounter rough times. You'll find His grace to be sufficient (2 Corinthians 12:9) as you humbly submit yourself to seek to handle life's crises...*His* way.

Lesson 9

Seeing the Big Picture

Luke 2:1-7

ow, I know Bible historians tell us that Jesus was *not* born on December 25, and that the December holiday of Christmas came to us from pagan roots. But still this wintry season is a time when we can remember the birth of Christ. And what woman doesn't have memories tucked away in her mind and heart that center on this joyous season? It seems that we pay special attention to our home, to our family, and to others at Christmastime.

And there's no doubt that our spiritual awareness is heightened as the holiday season centers on the birth of "the little Lord Jesus." I know in our household we memorized "the Christmas story" from the Bible. Then, on Christmas Eve, our daughters would stand on the hearth and recite the story from memory.

You probably know "the Christmas story" too. It is well loved by many. And its words are well known. But, dear one, if you are not careful, you just might miss "the big picture." You might miss the sovereign working of God through the lives of big government officials and little people who humbly obeyed the Lord.

Now let's carefully comb through this beloved story's facts.

From the Heart of God's Word...

1. Before we dive into new facts, how did Mary's visit with Elizabeth end in Luke 1:56?

2. Now read Luke 2:1-7. Who was the ruler "in those days," and what was his decree (verse 1)?

   How did this affect the people (verse 3)?

3. How did this decree affect Mary and Joseph (verses 4-5)?

   Describe Mary and Joseph's trip (verse 4).

   Also describe Mary's condition (verse 5).

4. What happened while Mary and Joseph were in Bethlehem (verses 6-7)?

   Describe the details of their baby's birth (verse 7).

From Your Heart...

- *The Place*—What did the prophet Micah predict in Micah 5:2?

  How did Caesar Augustus's decree help to bring about the fulfillment of Micah's prophecy?

- *The People*—What do you learn about Joseph's character from these verses?

  What lesson in character would you like to "take away" from his example?

  And what do you learn about Mary's character from these verses?

  What lesson in character would you like to "take away" from her example?

- *The Powers*—What does 1 Peter 2:13-15 teach us about obeying the government? Answer...and then ponder these observations.

*T*he twist in the story is, of course, that it is the very pagan authorities who are responsible for bringing Jesus to Bethlehem. Caesar...unknowingly becomes the servant of God's purpose. The promise is fulfilled through the actions of the unlikeliest of people. For God is Lord of all the earth and there is no power not under his authority....[11]

How does Proverbs 21:1 confirm the above statement that "there is no power not under God's authority"?

• *The Plan*—How did Mary and Joseph's obedience to the official decree fit into God's plan for the appearing of His Son and the redemption of mankind (Luke 2:6 and Micah 5:2)?

What do these scriptures teach us about our obedience and God's will?

Psalm 37:23—

Proverbs 16:9—

Proverbs 20:24—

• *The Price*—It's obvious that the trip to Bethlehem was a hardship for both Mary and Joseph. Imagine! Seventy to eighty miles of winding paths, rocky roads, and steep mountainous terrain! And imagine being almost full term in a pregnancy! And then imagine arriving...with no place to stay! And one more imagine—imagine giving birth away from home and family...and in a cave or stable, a place filled with animals *and* their smells! How much hardship and inconvenience are you willing to endure as God's instrument? Share a few details about the last time you really paid a price to do what was right.

Nurturing a Heart of Humility

Precious woman after God's own heart, Jesus Christ here in this passage is teaching us about true humility. Here we are witnessing the submission of Jesus Christ, God the Son, to birth! Think on it!

Now, what happens when you and I nurture a heart of humility? What happens when we humbly submit ourselves to others? To a husband? To a government? To authorities? To God's movement and directing in our life? God's Word says,

> ~ *The humble He guides in justice, and*
> *the humble He teaches His way.* ~
> (Psalm 25:9)

Like Mary and Joseph, two humble "little" people, we must live each day by faith and in humility, trusting that God is in charge of the "big" picture.

Responding to the Savior

Luke 2:8-20

*O*ther than precious family memories of Christmases gone by, today's verses remind me of the one year that I taught in a preschool. My fondest memory of that year was the annual Christmas program. These little ones had worked all year memorizing "the Christmas story" from Luke 2. On the evening of our program, they (as only three- and four-year-olds can do!) sweetly recited the words from the Bible that tell us of God's announcement of His best gift to the world. And, of course, when the darlings were done, everyone responded with thunderous applause!

Now read on and see how some others responded as the real Christmas story unfolded.

From the Heart of God's Word...

1. Luke 2:8-14—Whom do we first meet in this pastoral scene and what are they doing (verse 8)?

   In the darkness of an ordinary night, what extraordinary and dazzling miracle occurred (verse 9)?

   Briefly, what was the message delivered in...

   ...verse 10—

   ...verse 11—

   ...verse 12—

> *G*reat is the mystery of godliness:
> God was manifested in the flesh
> (1 Timothy 3:16).

   And what was the event of verses 13-14?

2. Luke 2:15-20—Don't you think such a miraculous scene requires a response?! What did the witnesses of such wonder do next (verse 15)?

   And how was their response rewarded (verse 16)?

And how did they respond to what they saw (verses 17 and 20)?

And what was the response of others (verse 18)?

And now for Mary—what was her response to all that she heard (verse 19)?

From Your Heart...

Revelation and responses! That's what these two scenes seem to depict.

- *Revelation*—What are some of the prophecies of the anticipated Messiah that were fulfilled with the arrival of the baby Jesus?

  Isaiah 7:14—

  Isaiah 9:6—

  Matthew 1:21—

  Luke 1:35—

- *Response of the shepherds*—These poor, simple folk, who were deemed to be unclean and unfit according to the law of God, were chosen by God to be the first to hear His announcement of His Son! And their response certainly sets a good example for us to follow.

✓ They received the message of God.

✓ They responded immediately in obedience.

✓ They told others.

Evaluate your response to God's Word, to God's revelation. Do you tend to respond...

...with instant obedience...or do you delay?

...by sharing with others...or do you keep spiritual truth to yourself?

- *Response of the angels*—A chorus of angels joined the first lone angel and gave an anthem of praise. Tens of thousands of angels met together to chant glory to God.[12] As one preacher noted,

> *W*hen Christ was born, midnight gloom lightened into midday brightness.... Heaven's choir came down to sing when Heaven's King came down to save.[13]

- *Response of your heart*—Have you yet responded to the "glad tidings" of the Savior? And are you sharing the good news with others?

Nurturing a Heart of Humility

And now for Mary's response! The Bible says she "kept" the words the shepherds shared about this wondrous, miraculous night and "pondered them in her heart."

As with all good things, the story of the Savior's birth grew dim in the minds of men with the passing of the years. Mary, however, did not forget. In fact, Luke's account is attributed to Mary's memories.

In the end, Mary's faith still sustained her, and the last picture we have of Mary is in the upper room with the 120 faithful believers…praying (Acts 1:14).

May Mary's response be true of your life and posture as well. May you and I continue to humbly "ponder" the things of God and to respond with adoration and wonder to the revelation of Jesus Christ.

Now, take a few minutes and praise God for His unspeakable gift of Jesus Christ. "Hallelujah, what a Savior!"

Lesson 11

Fulfilling God's Will

Luke 2:21-24

God never makes a mistake. And He certainly didn't make one when He chose the humble Mary to be the mother of His Son!

The responsibility of raising Jesus, the Righteous Branch of David, called for righteous parents who followed God's law. And, as these few verses in Luke 2 show us, Mary and Joseph clearly met that criterion.

The four verses that make up our lesson today address the rituals prescribed for newborn infants. Let's see how Mary and Joseph—a couple after God's own heart—completely fulfilled all God's will as written in the law of the Lord.

From the Heart of God's Word...

1. What took place eight days after the birth of Mary's Son?

   And what name was the infant given and why?

2. Mary and Joseph were faithful to take the next step of obedience called for in God's law. What was that step (verses 22-23)?

3. At that time, yet another criterion of the law was fulfilled. What was it (verse 24)?

From Your Heart...

In these few verses the law of the Lord—and its fulfill-ment—is mentioned three times.

- First, Jesus was circumcised exactly eight days after His birth, just as God's law required. What does Leviticus 12:3 require of Jewish parents?

  Also at this time, the child's name was given. The name commanded by the angel was then officially given to the infant. What does this indicate about Mary and Joseph?

- Second, Mary's purification after childbirth took place exactly 40 days after the birth of her male child. Briefly distill the requirements stated in God's law in Leviticus 12:2-5.

And what did Leviticus 12:6-8 then command of new parents?

We noted earlier that Mary was poor. What was the normal sacrifice, and how does the offering of a pair of turtledoves or pigeons further indicate the poverty of Mary and Joseph?

• Third, Mary presented Jesus, her firstborn son, to the Lord. How did this exactly fulfill the criterion of God's law according to Exodus 13:2?

• This Bible study series carries the banner, "A Woman After God's Own Heart." How is a man [or woman] after God's own heart defined in Acts 13:22?

Now, how do the four verses that make up our lesson today show us the righteous character of both Mary and Joseph?

What activities in your life are revealing *your* righteous character, your willingness to fulfill all God's will according to His Word? And, dear one, if something is lacking, what will you do right this minute(!) to get back on the righteous path of humble obedience?

*G*od uses broken things: broken soil and broken clouds to produce grain; broken grain to produce bread; broken bread to feed our bodies. He wants our stubbornness broken into humble obedience.[14]

- How does the Word of God define obedience in these scriptures?

John 14:15—

John 14:23-24—

John 15:10—

1 John 2:29—

As you think about these truths, what do you learn about the relationship between obedience to the Word of God and love for Jesus Christ?

Nurturing a Heart of Humility

In Mary we see the kind of woman God delights in—a woman after His own heart, a woman willing to do all His will. Only a woman intent on nurturing a heart of humility would even attempt the kind of obedience we see in Mary in this lesson!

It is true that, because of Jesus Christ's perfect fulfillment of God's law, we live in the age of God's marvelous grace. However, our obedience and wholehearted commitment to walking humbly in the ways of the Lord are still essential. Are you one who follows after God by walking in His ways? Spend time with the Lord now and affirm your desire to be, like Mary, a woman after God's own heart, a woman who fulfills all His will.

Living in Faith

Luke 2:25-35

*N*one of us knows exactly what the future holds. However, God allowed Mary a hint about what awaited her.

It's true that Mary was highly favored by God and greatly blessed to be the mother of His Son. But, as we glimpse today, this privilege brought with it real agony. Her joy would be mingled with sorrow—a sword would pierce her soul.

Let's learn now what another righteous person—the elderly Simeon—foretold regarding not only Mary's Son, but Mary as well.

From the Heart of God's Word...

1. To refresh your memory of the events leading up to today's passage of Scripture, review the facts of Luke 2:21-24.

2. *Simeon*—As we meet Simeon, how is he described (Luke 1:25)?

   What had God revealed to Simeon (verse 26)?

   While he was in the temple at Jerusalem, who also came to the temple and why (verse 27)?

3. *Jesus*—As Simeon took the infant into his arms, the Holy Spirit moved him to prophesy. How did Simeon describe the baby in...

   ...verse 30—

   ...verse 31—

   ...verse 32—

   ...verse 34—

4. *Mary*—When Simeon finished his prophecy regarding the infant, he turned to Mary. What words did he speak in verse 35...

...about her baby?

...about her?

From Your Heart...

Beloved, what an encounter this was! Four righteous and just people of God—Simeon (Luke 1:25), Mary (Luke 1:30), Joseph (Matthew 1:19), and, of course, the little Lord Jesus (Jeremiah 23:5)—all meeting up in the temple of God. Imagine the scene!

- *Simeon*—What can we learn from Simeon's lifestyle of faith as he expectantly waited for the Messiah?

Make notes on these verses. Then summarize what they teach us about a lifestyle of faith.

John 20:29—

Hebrews 11:1—

1 Peter 1:8—

1 John 3:2—

Summary—

- *Jesus*—Notice again how Simeon described our Savior in verses 29-34. He blessed and praised God for the infant who was "the Consolation of Israel," the Messiah who would comfort His people (Isaiah 40:1). What can we learn from Simeon's response of praise and about a lifestyle of praising God?

- *Mary*—We will never fully know the depth or degree of Mary's anguish, but Simeon's choice of words paints a gruesome picture. The word he used for *sword* is the same word found in the Old Testament to describe the giant Goliath's large, broad sword (1 Samuel 17:51). The pain Mary would know when her son was nailed to the cross would be like the pain inflicted by a huge and cruel weapon.

What does John 19:25 say about the fulfillment of Simeon's prophecy?

Nurturing a Heart of Humility

In humble and faithful expectation, Simeon (along with Mary and Joseph) had waited for the day when God would console and comfort His people. And on this one glorious day that began like any other day, God revealed to Simeon that, indeed, his eyes had seen, in the baby Jesus, the Messiah, God's Anointed King. At last, with the babe—the reality of the promise—in his arms, Simeon's full heart burst forth in humble praise and recognition of God's absolute sovereignty. His life of faith had been rewarded! He then blessed

God profusely for the privilege of seeing the Messiah and for God's plan of redemption for the world through Jesus Christ. And Mary, dear Mary. She had come in humble obedience to offer the sacrifice of the poor. And on this one day, one that began with such joy, God revealed through Simeon that sorrow was on its way...that Mary, too, like her Son, the Man of Sorrows (Isaiah 53:3), would suffer pain.

Yes, Simeon had lived in faith, hoping, praying, and now, seeing the Messiah. Now Mary must live in faith as she began that path of sorrows that would lead to the cross. As we said at the outset of this lesson, none of us knows what the future holds. But we do know, don't we, that whatever is forthcoming will require living in faith. That's what being a woman after God's own heart is all about.

Why not take a few minutes to read through all of Hebrews 11? Marvel at many who lived in faith!

Lesson 13

Serving the Lord

*T*oday we meet Anna, a woman whose life was touched by darkness. Her own dear husband had died after only seven years of marriage. In the intervening years, 84-year-old Anna had daily "lifted up her eyes to the hills" (Psalm 121:1) and looked for help and redemption from the Lord. Then, on one particular day, the Light of the world entered the temple of the Lord where Anna was devoutly serving the Lord. Mary arrived, carrying the long-awaited Christ Child in her arms—the One who would dispel the world's darkness. Anna was there...and her life—and yours!—would never be the same!

From the Heart of God's Word...

The Bible does not actually refer to Anna as a "righteous" person. But I think you'll agree that she, too, like Simeon, Mary, and Joseph, was someone quite special. She, like they, was a godly person who, in spite of the present low spiritual condition in the nation of Israel, was faithfully serving the Lord while looking for God to deliver His people.

1. First review the setting for Anna's story by looking again at Luke 2:21-35.

2. As we meet Anna now, what rather long list of facts do we learn about her in verse 36?

3. The description of Anna's devoutness continues in verse 37. Continue your list of details about her life here.

4. What happened in verse 38, and how did Anna respond?

From Your Heart...

- *Anna, the prophetess*—Very few women in the Bible are called a prophetess by God. A prophetess was the female equivalent of a prophet, one who was divinely inspired to communicate God's will to His people and to disclose the future to them.[15] What other prophetesses do we meet in...

...Exodus 15:20?

...Judges 4:4-7?

...2 Kings 22:14?

...Acts 21:9?

- *Anna, the widow*—How might Anna have been tempted to live her lonely life, and how did she choose to live it instead?

How does Anna's *life of service* set a good example for you and me as women as we contemplate the approaching days and decades?

Look at 1 Timothy 5:5. How do you see Anna "trusting in God"? And how does Anna's *life of trust* set a good example for you?

- *Anna, the worshiper*—What spiritual disciplines do you observe in Anna's godly life?

And how does she set an example of piety for us?

Also how does she model the godly "older woman" spoken of in Titus 2:3, setting yet another good example for us?

- *Anna, the witness*—Faith is described in the Bible as "the substance of things hoped for, the evidence of things not seen" (Hebrews 11:1). Anna's long-term faith was definitely rewarded! How can you take a page out of Anna's, so to speak?

- *Anna, the encourager*—Anna's life may have been sad and lonely. Yet she teaches us a valuable lesson in encouraging one another. How do you think Mary, who had just heard Simeon's prophecy (please see again Luke 1:35) regarding the baby in her arms, may have been encouraged by Anna's exultation?

Are you one who seeks to lift up, encourage, and restore those who are cast down? Better yet, note three things you can do to be *more* of this kind of encourager.

To speak a timely word of ever-burning faith in God to those who are weary is indeed a divine art!

Nurturing a Heart of Humility

As you can see, a life of faith has many aspects! All that we know about Anna schools us in humility! In the widow Anna we witness a life of steadfast hope and faithful worship, prayer, and service. Anna shows you and me vividly, dear one, the winning combination of qualities that make up a heart of humility!

Lesson 14

Seeking the Lord

Matthew 2:1-12

Are you a student of bumper stickers? Yes, I know some of them are awful! But there is one that sends a true message. It reads, "Wise men still seek Him." Nothing could sum up today's lesson any better!

From the Heart of God's Word...

1. Read Matthew 2:1-6—Name the persons we meet in verse 1.

Also note the cities mentioned (verse 1).

What was the visitors' query and why (verse 2)?

How did King Herod respond when he heard of their inquiry (verse 3)?

And what action did he take as a result (verses 3-4)?

How did the priests and scribes answer Herod (verses 5-6)?

What did Micah 5:2 predict?

2. Read Matthew 2:7-9—Once Herod had rounded up the wise men, what did he do (verses 7-8)?

How did the wise men respond to Herod's request (verse 9)?

And how were they guided (verses 9-10)?

3. Read Matthew 2:11-12—When their mission was accomplished, what did the wise men then do (verse 11)?

What exciting, miraculous event happened next (verse 12)?

And how did the wise men respond (verse 12)?

From Your Heart...

- *The wise men*—Make a list of the noble traits you observe in these true seekers of the Lord. Then write out what impresses you the most about them and why.

For your information, these men journeyed from "the East," literally "from the rising of the sun,"[16] an arduous trek that possibly covered thousands of miles and required many months.

What woman made a similar trip (read 1 Kings 10:1-13)?

- *Herod*—What title is ascribed to Herod in Matthew 2:1, and who did the wise men say they were seeking in verse 2? What ignoble traits do you observe in Herod?

- *The priests and scribes*—What prideful traits do you observe in this group that made up the intelligentsia of their day? Then state how such traits send a warning to us today.

Just a thought: The religious leaders in Jerusalem knew *where* the Messiah was to be born...but they didn't know *when*. The wise men from the East, on the other hand, knew *when*...but not *where*. Once these two groups of "wise men" shared their information, for some reason the "wise men" from Jerusalem did not travel the five miles to Bethlehem to witness the miracle of God-in-flesh...while the "wise men" from the East, with complete information, completed their quest.

- *Mary and Joseph*—Note where this couple and the "child king" are now residing (verse 11). Then read the following observations about their little Son:

The Great Troublemaker

When Jesus was born into our world, people immediately began to react. His presence did not soothe and comfort people; instead, it startled and disturbed them. In some, he awakened spiritual longings; in others, fear and insecurity. If it is true that God entered our world when Jesus was born, we dare not sit idly by ignoring and rationalizing our inaction. We must acknowledge Jesus as the rightful King of our lives. He did not stay in the manger.[17]

- *God's guidance*—Did you note the miracles in these few verses? List them here and briefly tell how God used each miracle—including the miracle of the facts revealed in His Word—to direct and protect.

Nurturing a Heart of Humility

In our day of self-made, self-contained, "put together," "I'm my own person" self-seekers, it's refreshing to meet a band of humble God-seekers. Whatever wealth and status these wise men from the East possessed in their homeland, they were still humble enough to follow after a star and seek the one born "King of the Jews." They were still humble enough to undertake a long and grueling trip to find such a One. They were still humble enough to load their camels with riches to bestow upon such a Personage. They were still humble enough to worship a child King.

Are you a humble God-seeker? What sacrifices are you making to seek the Lord, to find the truth?

Lesson 15

Obeying the Lord

Matthew 2:13-23

~ Obedience is the fruit of faith. ~

~ Obedience to God
is the most infallible evidence
of sincere and supreme love to Him. ~

ow would you describe your obedience to God's direction in your life? Are you quick to follow...or do you hem, haw, and hesitate, question and rationalize, "Wait until later"?

Let's look at how the urgent obedience of one man was key to God's directing and protecting of that man and his loved ones.

From the Heart of God's Word...

1. Read again Matthew 2:1-12 to catch up with where today's lesson begins.

2. Now read Matthew 2:13-15. After the wise men left the house of Mary and Joseph and Jesus, what miracle occurred (verse 13)?

   What message was sent to Joseph and why (verse 13)?

   How did Joseph respond and when (verse 14)?

   How long did Joseph and his family remain in Egypt and why (verse 15)?

3. Read Matthew 2:16-18. Meanwhile, Herod was having his own problems. What had happened, and how did he respond (verse 16)?

   What prophecy did Herod's actions unknowingly fulfill (verses 17-18)?

4. Read Matthew 2:19-23. When Herod died, what miracle occurred next (verse 19)?

   And what was the message (verse 20)?

And how did Joseph respond (verse 21)?

How did Joseph determine where to take his family (verses 22-23)?

What prophecy did Joseph's actions unknowingly fulfill (verse 23)?

From Your Heart...

• *Herod*—Characterize this man and his actions. Then summarize your thoughts into a statement.

Now take note of Jeremiah 31:15, a prophecy fulfilled in these eleven verses.

Think About It...

*E*ven before the tiny baby could speak, the worldly powers, led by Satan himself, were moving against him. Herod, a ruthless king who had killed three of his own sons to secure his power, was afraid of losing that power, so he embarked on a plan to kill the tiny child who had been born "king of the Jews." In his madness, Herod murdered innocent children, hoping to kill this one child. Herod stained his hands with blood, but he did not harm Jesus. No one can thwart God's plans.[18]

• *Joseph*—Characterize this man and his actions. What lessons in humility can you learn from him?

Now look up Hosea 11:1, another prophecy fulfilled in this passage.

• *Mary*—Characterize Mary's willingness to be led by her husband.

What lessons in humility and/or submission can you learn from her?

What would you have done?

• *God*—In what ways do you see God at work in and through the people in this passage?

Nurturing a Heart of Humility

As we've already noted in this Bible study, a man or woman after God's own heart is defined in Acts 13:22 as one who will fulfill all God's will. This makes obedience key to being a woman after God's own heart!

And our obedience is synonymous with humility. Why? Because you and I cannot obey and will not obey the Lord without this prized flower of humility. And that, dear one, makes it awfully important to nurture a heart of humility. You see, a woman with a heart of humility will readily obey the Lord.

Perhaps you don't sense the importance of urgent obedience. Perhaps you are one who thinks, "Oh, I'll get around to it one of these days." Imagine what might have occurred if Joseph had approached obedience with such a self-centered, light-hearted attitude! But no. Joseph, the humble carpenter, was a man after God's own heart. And Joseph obeyed God's commands explicitly, immediately, and without question. Joseph's obedience, humanly speaking, saved the baby Jesus, who could then live a sinless life and die, not at Herod's hand, but according to the perfect plan of God.

Beloved, are there commands from the Lord you need to obey today? Oh, please don't wait! Just do it!

*esson 16

Growing in Grace

*I*f you've ever read through the book of Philippians, I'm sure you, too, have been moved by verses 6-7 in Philippians 2. They read:

> [...Christ Jesus,] who, being in the form of God, did not consider it robbery to be equal with God, but made Himself of no reputation, taking the form of a servant, and coming in the likeness of men.

Today, as we look at a short (two verses!) account of Jesus' childhood, you'll see Jesus growing up in a small, humble town of no (or even bad!) reputation, a place of obscurity and reproach. You'll also see Him maturing and developing in the humble home of Mary and Joseph just like any other boy or girl, utterly unrecognizable as the Christ.

But in the process of growing up, you'll witness Jesus growing in grace and in favor with God.

From the Heart of God's Word...

As we step into this glimpse of about a decade of quiet home life, keep in mind that Luke summarized events and moved on. Here in Luke 2 he omitted Joseph's family's stay in Bethlehem, the visit of the wise men from the East, and their flight to Egypt.[19]

1. Read Luke 2:39-40. How does verse 39 begin?

   Scan now Luke 2:21-24 and note what "all" the "things" were that Joseph and Mary performed according to the law.

2. When all these things were accomplished, where did the little family go (verse 39)?

3. Make a list of the lovely phrases that describe the next years of Jesus' life in verse 40.

From Your Heart...

Throughout Luke's gospel, Luke, a physician, presents Jesus in His humanity, as Christ, the Man. Here Luke describes Jesus' growing up and maturing in terms of development. Jesus had a normal childhood (Isaiah 53:2a) and progressed naturally from being an infant...to a toddler...to a young child. Evidently no one thought of Him as unusual or anything more than a common boy. The people of His day certainly did not point to Him and exclaim, "There is God!"[20] Instead, Jesus was observed to grow physically and mentally.

Jesus grew physically—"Grew" refers to physical growth.

Jesus grew in wisdom—"Filled with wisdom" refers to His intellectual growth.

Jesus "grew in grace"—The grace of God suggests that divine favor rested manifestly and increasingly upon Jesus.[21] Jesus was the object of "the favor of God."

- Compare this description of Jesus' growth and maturity with that of His cousin in Luke 1:80. What similarities and differences do you notice?

- If you are a parent, or if you work with little ones, how do these scriptures help you to determine the importance and emphasis of your efforts?

   2 Timothy 1:5—

   2 Timothy 3:15—

- And what does 2 Peter 3:18 say to you and me?

• Now let's check out your own growth, your own balanced, well-rounded health and development.

—*Physical*—You've probably already matured in the physical area of life and have now reached another growth problem—"the battle of the bulge"! What is God's challenge to you in...

...1 Corinthians 9:27?

...1 Timothy 4:8?

—*Spiritual*—As God, Jesus needed only to grow in human wisdom. You and I, however, must grow spiritually as well as mentally. A familiar children's song gives us several clues about growing spiritually: "Read your Bible, pray every day, and you'll grow, grow, grow!" How are you doing in these two very basic requirements for spiritual growth?

—*Mental*—Many Christians grow in wisdom every day by reading the chapter of Proverbs that corresponds with the day's date. Jot down the day of the month here: _____ Next read that chapter of Proverbs and check here when you are done. _____ Now...make this practice a life habit. It only takes about two minutes a day!

Nurturing a Heart of Humility

And finally, *grace*...wonderful grace! As someone has noted,

> Humility is a bag into which Christ puts the riches of His grace. The one infallible test of our holiness will be the humility before God and men which marks us. Humility is the bloom and the beauty of holiness. The chief mark of counterfeit holiness is a lack of humility.[22]

May you and I, dear precious friend, ever be found increasing and growing in His grace and in the knowledge of Him as we nurture a heart of humility!

Lesson 17

Establishing Priorities

More than 25 years ago, Jim and I were challenged to establish some serious priorities for our lives as Christians. Both of us still vividly recall the Sunday when we sat down at our dining table...pens and paper in hand... while our preschoolers napped. After prayerfully asking God for His guidance, we spent the entire afternoon establishing a set of life priorities. Our sole desire was (and still is!) to place God and His Word at the center of our lives.

Today as a couple we are still attempting to live by those priorities based on the commands of Scripture. And, praise God, the intervening quarter century has been one of spiritual growth, family development (and expansion—including five grandchildren!), and meaningful ministry. We can only thank Him for His marvelous grace!

And now, dear seeker of His heart, let's pay careful attention as we inspect the lives of two who established godly priorities and sought to obey God's Word.

From the Heart of God's Word...

1. Luke 2:41-42—Just as we've seen throughout our study of Mary and Joseph, here again we find them fulfilling the prescribed worship called for in the law of Moses. What are they doing in verse 41?

   And how old was Jesus, according to verse 42?

2. Luke 2:43-45—Describe what happened when their time in Jerusalem was over (verse 43).

   And describe what happened as they journeyed home (verse 44).

   What did Mary and Joseph eventually do (verse 45)?

3. Luke 2:46-50—Finally(!) Jesus was found! What did it appear He had been doing for the past three days (verse 46)?

   What was the response of all who heard Jesus' interactions (verse 47)?

What was the response of Jesus' parents when they found Him, and what did Mary say to Him (verse 48)?

And what was Jesus' response to His parents (verse 49)?

How did Mary and Joseph handle Jesus' answer (verse 50)?

From Your Heart...

• *Home life*—What insights does Luke 1:39-42 give us about Jesus' home life and His parents' priorities?

Could the same be said of your home life? Why or why not? Do you need to make any changes in your priorities?

• *Trip*—Read Exodus 13:3-10. Why was this group of family and friends so faithful to make this annual trip from Nazareth to Jerusalem? And what does this say about their priorities and their obedience to God's Word?

In what ways do you (and your family) honor and obey God's commands to worship?

* *Temple*—Here we witness the boy Jesus interacting with the religious teachers of the day. What does Jesus' interest in the temple discussion reveal about Him?

* *Announcement*—Of course Jesus' parents worried! (Wouldn't you?) But Jesus viewed the situation differently from His parents. How did His famous response—the first recorded words of the Messiah (verse 49)—reveal His understanding of the priorities of His life?

(Just a note—Bible scholars teach us that it is clear from Jesus' answer concerning "His Father" that Jesus, even at the age of 12, was deeply conscious of the unique relation between Himself and His Father in heaven.[23])

Nurturing a Heart of Humility

Mary and Joseph were a couple who nurtured hearts of humility. How do we know that? Because they had established godly priorities for their lives from the beginning. God was *first* in their lives...and God was *all* in their lives. Both Mary and Joseph were godly singles...who became a godly couple...who became godly parents. Today's scene portrays them going about the business of humbly living by the godly priorities and focus they had maintained all their lives.

We only get a brief glimpse of the next 20 years of Mary's life. But in the end, her established priorities were what sustained her...through the probable death of her husband Joseph, through the years of ridicule over the questionable details of her Son's conception and birth, and through those final days leading up to her standing at the foot of the cross of Jesus (John 19:25).

Now...what are the priorities by which you live *your* life? Are they based on obedience to God's Word and God's commands? Do you perhaps need to spend time with the Lord establishing or adjusting your priorities so that you can more readily obey the commands of God as this godly couple did?

~ Seek first the kingdom of God
and His righteousness,
and all these things shall be added to you. ~
Matthew 6:33

esson 18

Living at Home

Luke 2:51-52

ome is where the heart is." (I'm sure you've heard this phrase before!) True, it's a nice sentiment. But home is not only where *your* heart is as a homemaker. Home is also the heart, the hub, and the place where you and I as women after God's own heart can exert our influence on *others* by centering home life on what is worthwhile and possesses eternal value.

In today's lesson we'll focus on Mary's heart and home. Both provided a place for God's Son to live while being prepared for the ministry that was to come.

From the Heart of God's Word...

1. Quickly read again Luke 2:41-50. Then note the highlights of this portion of Scripture below.

2. Now read Luke 2:51. What do you learn about...

   ...Jesus?

   ...Mary?

   As you think about Luke 2:46-47, what makes verse 51 so noteworthy?

   Also, compare Mary's response in verse 51 to that in Luke 2:19. What does this habit suggest to us about Mary?

3. Finally, read Luke 2:52. For your information, Luke 2:39-52 contains all we know of Jesus' growing-up years, all we know of His boyhood, all we know of His years of living at home. Compare verse 52 to verse 40. What picture do they sketch of Jesus' growth and development?

From Your Heart...

- *Mary, the mom*—Every mom has stored up a museum of memories in her heart. The Gospel of Luke is, so to speak, Mary's photo album of Jesus' days of living at home. Luke drew his information for his gospel account of the life of Christ from Mary's memories. Mary was also...

- *Mary, the homemaker*—Let's look at the home Mary built (see Proverbs 14:1). Every child thrives in a godly home—even Jesus, the Son of God! Surely Mary's home was built on love and on biblical childraising principles. What are a few of these principles for childraising that the Bible gives to parents?

Deuteronomy 6:6-7—

Proverbs 1:8—

Proverbs 6:20—

Ephesians 6:4—

So, how did Jesus grow up? What kind of home did Mary and Joseph provide? In short, it was a normal home life.

✓ Jesus had, as today's popular label puts it, a "stay-at-home mom" in Mary.

✓ Jesus had in Joseph a father who worked as a carpenter (see Matthew 13:55). This means Jesus learned to be a carpenter (Mark 6:3). (And, just for our information, Luke 2:51 is the last reference to Joseph in the Bible, indicating he may have died before Jesus' public ministry began at about age 30.)

✓ Jesus subjected Himself to His earthly mother and father...in subjection to the law handed down by His heavenly Father. What did the law of Moses require in...

...Exodus 20:12?

...Deuteronomy 5:16?

✓ Jesus had at least six siblings. How many can you name from Matthew 13:55-56 and Mark 6:3?

Now let's focus on you and your heart...and what it's like living in your home!

- *You, the mom*—Do you have children? If so, what is your God-given assignment found in Titus 2:4?

- *You, the homemaker*—And what is your God-given assignment according to Titus 2:5?

- *Your assignment*—On a piece of paper, write out a few goals that will make this acrostic true of living in your home. Post your list where you'll see it, and check your progress.

> **H** onor the Lord in your home.
> **O** wn your role as a homemaker.
> **M** ake your house a home.
> **E** stablish lasting family memories.

Nurturing a Heart of Humility

Home, dear one, is the greatest place for you and me as women after God's own heart to nurture a heart of humility. Why? Because at home we are not "paid professionals." We are moms and homemakers going about the business of obeying God's commands to us in these two vital areas. Home is a place where you and I live out God's priority of humbly and constantly serving others—even "little people"!—to ensure that living at home is truly a…

Home, sweet home,
where each lives for the other, and
all live for God.

Lesson 19

Responding to Jesus

*E*very woman has attended or been a part of a wedding (...maybe even more weddings than she's wished!). In my case, weddings consumed two years of my life as my two daughters married one year to the day apart! And I'll *never* know all that went on in the church kitchen or behind the scenes as my friends "managed" both weddings and receptions for me so I could graciously (and obliviously!) mingle with our cherished guests. Perhaps today's lesson will bring to mind a few weddings—and a few wedding bloopers and blunders—that you've tried hard to forget!

Today we witness a wedding—a common, ordinary occurrence. And, sure enough, a problem arose. Fortunately, Someone was there to effect a solution. In fact, the solution was so wondrous and glorious that it demanded a response from all present...and demands a response from you and me.

From the Heart of God's Word...

1. *John 2:1-3—The record.* What do we learn about the setting for this scene from verses 1 and 2?

   What did Mary report to Jesus (verse 3)?

2. *John 2:4—The reply.* Write out Jesus' reply here.

3. *John 2:5—The response.* How did Mary humbly handle Jesus' reply?

4. *John 2:6-10—The revelation.* In your own words, describe the unfolding of the miracle in...

   ...verses 6-7—

   ...verses 8-10—

5. *John 2:11-12—The reason and aftermath.* According to verse 11, what was the purpose of this first miracle performed by Jesus?

   What effect did the miracle have on Jesus' disciples (verse 11)?

   How does this scene end (verse 12)?

From Your Heart...

Jesus is now about 30 years old (Luke 3:23). He has already been baptized by John the Baptist and has called His first disciples to follow Him (John 1:29-50). Also bear in mind that Joseph, Mary's husband, has possibly already died. Jesus lived on a divine schedule—the Father's schedule—and Mary is having to once again adapt to that schedule (Luke 2:49). Let's inspect the many responses to Jesus in this glorious scene.

- *Mary*—As she faced the problem that arose at the wedding, Mary turned to Jesus for help. She trusted Him to handle the problem. Beloved, what is your Number One problem today? And how does Mary's response to her problem instruct you regarding yours?

Just a note of explanation—Jesus' reply to Mary does not imply disrespect. Rather, Jesus wanted His mother to understand that He was on a heavenly timetable. He would do what the Father wanted Him to do...when the Father wanted Him to do it.

What did Mary then do (verse 5)?

- *The Servants*—What happens when the servants obey Jesus' command?

Jesus could have caused the pots to become miraculously filled...but He graciously allowed these servants to participate in the work of God. In the end, their obedience afforded them a private peek into the power and Person of God!

Like these servants, we would do well to do "whatever He says to you" (John 2:5)! What is God asking you to do today...

...in your spiritual growth?

...in your family relationships?

...in your home?

...in your ministry?

...in your job?

• *The Host*—How does the "master of ceremonies" respond? And whom does he call and credit?

Have you ever done a good deed that went unnoticed? Have you ever done something good...only to have someone else receive the credit? How does such an occurrence give humility an opportunity to grow in our hearts?

> *T*he humble man [or woman] feels no jealousy or envy. He can praise God when others are preferred and blessed before him. He can bear to hear others praised while he is forgotten because...he has received the spirit of Jesus, who pleased not Himself, and Who sought not His own honor.[24]

- *The Brothers*—Perhaps Jesus' brothers never knew about the miracle that took place in Cana. What does John 7:5 tell us about them?

- *The Disciples*—In contrast to His own brothers, how did the disciples respond to Jesus (verse 11)?

- *You*—Have you responded to Jesus Christ in the way that the disciples did? Or is yours more like the response of His own siblings? Please explain your answer.

Nurturing a Heart of Humility

Humility, dear heart-sister, is like a flower with its head hung low. Note well the beautiful bouquet of humility arranged on that glorious day in Cana.

Jesus—quietly performed a miracle...which only a few knew about...and was content for someone else to receive the credit and praise for His goodness.

Mary—quietly and humbly accepted Jesus' mild reproof and reminder. She was also content to let Jesus handle the situation in His own way.

The servants—quietly and humbly obeyed Jesus. After all, to their knowledge He was merely the son of a woman who was helping out with a wedding. Yet they lived out the definition of a servant and obeyed without question.

Are you following in the humble steps of Jesus, Mary, and the servants? Are your responses to Jesus those of a woman who is nurturing a heart of humility?

esson 20

Belonging to God's Family
Matthew 12:46-50; Mark 3:31-35; Luke 8:19-21

*A*re you blessed to have a mother who is still living? If so, I'm sure you'll agree that in your mother's eyes, you're still a child. In fact, your mom is probably still treating you like a child! This seems to be a universal trait of mothers, even those behind great men!

Behind Every Great Man Is His Mother

*M*rs. Morse: "Sam, stop tapping your fingers on the table. It's driving me crazy!"

Mrs. Lindbergh: "Charles, can't you do anything by yourself?"

Mrs. Washington: "George never did have a head for money."

Mrs. Armstrong: "Neil has no more business taking flying lessons than the man on the moon."[25]

Certainly Mary was not in this category—and neither was Jesus! But she did have her motherly concerns.

Today we see Jesus, a man on a mission—indeed, in the *midst* of a mission. We also see Mary's heartfelt regard for her Son's well-being.

From the Heart of God's Word...

1. First read Mark 3:20-21. These verses establish the background for our current lesson. What do you learn here...

   ...about the crowd?

   ...about Jesus' ministry?

   ...about Jesus' "own people"?

2. Next read Matthew 12:46-50. Check here when done.

   ———

3. Now read Mark 3:31-35. What is the setting for this scene, according to verses 32 and 34?

   Who came along and interrupted this scene (verses 31-32)?

   And what did they want (verse 32)?

   How did Jesus respond (verses 33-34)?

And how did Jesus define His "new family" relationships (verse 35)?

4. Finally, read Luke 8:19-21. Do you learn anything new from this passage?

From Your Heart...

• *Your relationship to Jesus Christ*—According to Matthew 12:50 and Mark 3:35, what is the basis for a "family" relationship with Jesus?

What does Luke 8:21 say is the basis for a "family" relationship with Jesus?

After considering these criteria, what would you say about your relationship with Jesus? And what does this reveal about your attitude toward the will of God? Be honest. Also note what it is you must do to better meet His requirements.

• *Your relationship with others*—Many Christians have family and friends who do not understand their belief in and love for Jesus Christ. How does the Bible say humility helps in your relationships with others in...

...Exodus 20:12?

...Romans 12:18?

...Colossians 4:6?

...2 Timothy 2:24?

...1 Peter 3:1-2?

Are there any changes in your behavior that would make you a better witness for Christ? Note them here.

Nurturing a Heart of Humility

Spiritual relationships are as binding as physical ones. In fact, your spiritual relationship with God takes primacy over your physical, familial relationships.

So...what does it take to belong to the family of God, to be a faithful follower of Christ?

Following Jesus

The types of people who can have a relationship with Christ are those who do the Father's will. They listen, learn, believe, and follow. Obedience is the key to being part of God's family. Knowledge is not enough—the religious leaders had that and still missed Jesus. Following is not enough—the crowd did that but still didn't understand who Jesus was. Those who believe are brought into a family.[26]

What a sublime *lesson!* Jesus, of course, perfectly loved His family and friends. And, in the same way that He loved them, He also loves His followers. And what a sublime *truth!* That you and I can be related to Christ and belong to God's family!

As a line of poetry reads,

> Who serves my Father as a son
> is surely kin to me.[27]

Lesson 21

Rejecting the Truth

*W*hat thoughts come to mind when you hear the word "family"? Are yours warm, happy memories...or not so pleasant? Most people's family memories recall two kinds of events—the everyday life of meals and routines...and holidays.

The story in today's lesson of Jesus' return visit to His hometown sparked my thoughts about Jesus' family. So pardon me while I use the introduction to this lesson to discuss Mary as a mother—not only of Jesus, but of at least six other children. We've studied much about Mary's visit from the angel Gabriel, about the miracle of Jesus' conception, about her relationship with her husband, Joseph. By now we know much about the early days of her motherhood of Jesus—about Jesus' birth, the visits from the shepherds and the wise men from the East, about her flight to Egypt to save her Son's life. We've even looked at what her first decade of raising Jesus may have been like.

But Mary's responsibilities did not end with caring for her Son Jesus. No, many other children were born to Mary! Hers was a busy household—teeming with babies, toddlers, and teenagers. There were probably weddings...and probably even grandchildren.

I know this passage is about something much more serious than Mary's child-raising experiences, but it did seem like a good opportunity to think on what Mary's life was like.

Now...on to the serious scene at hand.

From the Heart of God's Word...

1. First read Luke 4:16-30. This passage describes Jesus' *first* return visit to His hometown of Nazareth after the beginning of His ministry. Briefly share what happened.

2. Now read Matthew 13:54-58. This is Jesus' *final* visit to His hometown of Nazareth. Tension has most definitely been building in Jesus' relationship with the townsfolk in Nazareth! What did Jesus do that triggered this tension (verse 54)?

As the townspeople ridiculed and wondered at Jesus' words and works, how did they "explain away" and "rationalize away" the obvious conclusion that Jesus was God in flesh, the long-awaited Messiah (verses 55-56)?

Describe the people's roll call of Jesus'...

...father—

...mother—

...brothers (name them)—

...sisters—

Be sure to note the additional information about Jesus given in Mark 6:3.

3. What do we learn about Jesus' brothers in John 7:5?

And what do we learn about Jesus' brothers in Acts 1:13-14?

4. What do we learn about Jesus' brother James in...

...Galatians 1:18-19?

...James 1:1?

And about Jesus' brother Jude in Jude 1?

5. In the end, what was the people's reaction to Jesus (Matthew 13:57)?

And what were Jesus' final words to the citizens of Nazareth (verse 57)?

From Your Heart...

* The people of Nazareth were about to receive a second chance to believe. Unfortunately, they again rejected the Lord. Why?

* How did others react and reject...

   ...Jesus in Matthew 27:18?

   ...Stephen in Acts 7:57-58?

   ...Paul in Acts 13:44-45?

   ...Paul in Acts 14:19?

   ...Paul in Acts 16:23-24?

* *Rejecting Christ*—How important is accepting Christ and the message of Christ, according to these verses?

John 14:6—

1 John 5:10—

Now read 1 John 5:11-12. Beloved, do you have the Son...or not? Do you have eternal life...or not? Remember that to reject the truth about Jesus means to reject eternal life and the Father, and to call God a liar (1 John 5:10)!

- *Rejecting instructions*—Can you think of *any* message of truth or instruction you are rejecting? Think about it. Then think about...

  ...Proverbs 1:7—

  ...Proverbs 12:15—

Nurturing a Heart of Humility

Now think about this. The people were offended at Jesus' message because of His humble status,

- ✓ because He was only a carpenter,
- ✓ because He was only the son of a carpenter,
- ✓ because He was related to a common family,
- ✓ because He was "just one of us."

In short, Jesus' family was a common, ordinary family. They were not educated. They were not teachers. They were not synagogue officials. They were not professionals. They were not wealthy.

And, dear one, this obviously describes Mary. She was someone average. Someone normal. Someone just like you and me—or perhaps even someone a little *less* like you and me in terms of education and opportunity.

Yes, Mary was an ordinary woman...whose life had centered on fulfilling God's will for her as a wife and a mother and a homemaker. Yet God worked through this ordinary woman to accomplish the *extra*ordinary—to bring His Son into this world!

And God worked through His Son, who seemed so ordinary that others missed the *extra*ordinary truth—He was God in flesh!

Don't make the same mistake the people of Mary's day and Mary's hometown did. Don't reject the truth, no matter how…or through whom…it comes!

Lesson 22

Heeding God's Word

One of these days I'm planning (Lord willing!) to create a Bible study for you and me—and other women after God's own heart—on the Gospel of Luke. Why Luke? Because Luke, more than any other gospel writer, shows us the most incidents that reveal the tenderness and love with which Jesus treated women. Through the eyes and pen of Luke, we also witness how women responded to Jesus.

Let's listen in now as Luke recalls for us one such instance. Today we meet a woman…who mentions another woman—Mary…and who receives, from the lips of Jesus, a truth that opened up the path to spiritual blessing, not only for her but also for you and me!

From the Heart of God's Word...

1. While Jesus was interacting with and answering a group of objectors, what happened (verse 27)?

   And what was said (verse 27)?

2. How did Jesus use this incident to teach a more important truth (verse 28)?

   According to Jesus, who is more blessed than one with a mere physical tie to Him (verse 28)?

   Once again, what two criteria does Jesus set forth for a spiritual relationship with Him (verse 28)?

   —

   —

From Your Heart...

- *Comparing*—Is this lesson and Jesus' message sounding familiar? If so, it's because we've already dealt with this truth. Look again at Luke 8:19-21. As you compare the two passages, how is the teaching in Luke 8 different from our present lesson?

And how is it similar?

In your own words, what is Jesus' message?

- *Hearing*—Jesus spoke of hearing the Word of God. List at least three means you have *available* to you for hearing the Word of God.

Now...on a regular daily basis, how are you *actively* hearing the Word of God? And what will you do to increase your hearing of it?

- *Heeding*—Jesus spoke also of *keeping* the Word of God, of heeding it with a heart of obedience. What do these verses say about hearing *and* heeding the Word of God?

James 1:22—

1 John 2:3-4—

1 John 2:28-29—

Can you think of any commands and teachings of Scripture that you know you are not presently heeding or obeying? And what will you do to wholeheartedly heed and obey them...starting right this minute?

- *Understanding*—Here are a few bits of information to help us with our understanding of this portion of Scripture.

  ✓ These words from Jesus in Luke 11 declare that "to hear the Word of God and keep it is to be more blessed than to be connected with Christ by the ties of flesh, and that to be the mother of Christ according to the flesh does not confer on any one greater honor and privileges than to believe and obey the Gospel."[28]

  ✓ Jesus here points out that a spiritual relationship to Him is far more important than a physical relationship. A relationship more meaningful than one through family ties is afforded to multitudes of others...if they obey the Word of God. As one teacher emphasizes, "This is a key point in Christ's thinking and teaching."[29]

Nurturing a Heart of Humility

As we finish this lesson by asking the question, "How can I nurture a heart of humility?" the answer is obvious, isn't it? We nurture a heart of humility by humbly hearing and humbly heeding the Word of God. Jesus makes it plain that we are to humbly bow our hearts and souls to the truth of His Word.

Do you want to be blessed? Do you want to enjoy a deep, spiritual relationship with Jesus Christ? Then realize, my dear reading friend, that hearing and heeding is the required response to Scripture. Your attitude toward God's Word is what is supremely important. Your response to Scripture opens the path to blessing.

Yes, Mary was blessed. Jesus never implied that she wasn't. As Luke reported, Mary was favored by God (Luke 1:28). But Mary was blessed because she heard and heeded the Word of God, a habit we've witnessed in her throughout this study. And you and I, dear one, are blessed, too, as we show forth the marks of belonging to Jesus, as we hear and heed His Word.

esson 23

Following Faithfully

*W*hat is faithfulness? It has been described in this way: "Faithfulness speaks of endurance, also a firmness of purpose, especially amid danger and calamities. It describes the faithful discharge of duties and undying devotion to persons and principles. It is the love which endures all things—difficulties, dangers, and differences."[30]

All of these elements, precious one, are present in the lesson at hand! Prepare to witness endurance in the midst of danger and calamity. Get ready to meet a circle of women—and one man!—who faithfully discharged their duties in undying devotion to a Son, to a Person, to a Friend—to our Lord Jesus Christ. Brace yourself for some definite difficulties and dangers!

From the Heart of God's Word...

1. John 19:25—Where does this disturbing scene take place?

   And who is present?

2. John 19:26—Who else was "at the cross"?

   (John's gospel reveals that this disciple was John, the writer of the Gospel of John and the one describing this scene for us.)

   What did Jesus say to Mary?

3. John 19:27—What did Jesus say to John?

   And what was the result of Jesus' instructions?

From Your Heart...

God truly gives us here a kaleidoscope of events to behold and emotions to review...and lessons to learn!

- *The cross*—Our hearts are deeply touched as we witness in this scene the crucifixion of our faithful Savior on a cross! The cross was an instrument of death, but it is now the symbol of life for us who believe in Jesus Christ, the

One who died on a cross for our sins. What does Romans 5:8 say about Christ's death on the cross?

• *The women*—Throughout Jesus' ministry, a number of women were faithful to follow and take care of Him. "At the cross" we meet some of these women. Let's look at two of them.

Scholars tell us that Jesus' mother's sister was probably Salome, the wife of Zebedee. Briefly, what else do we learn about her from Matthew 4:21-22 and Matthew 20:20-21?

Most women are familiar with Mary Magdalene. What was her relationship with Jesus, according to Luke 8:2-3?

Just a note—Mary Magdalene is the only woman at the cross who is mentioned in all four gospel accounts.

• *The disciple*—To our knowledge, only three men were willing to be identified with Jesus at the end—John, Nicodemus, and Joseph of Arimathea (John 19:38-42). Where were the other disciples (Matthew 26:56)?

And what do we know about John from Matthew 4:21-22?

What does this scene reveal about John's character? About his faithfulness?

- *The Son*—Jesus was the perfect Savior...and the perfect Son. As one has exclaimed regarding His thoughtfulness of His mother at a time of great pain, "What forgetfulness of self, what filial love, and to the 'mother' and 'son' what parting words!"[31]

What can you do today to follow in Jesus' steps and show your love for your family?

- *The mother*—Mary, the mother of Jesus, was personally present when the tragic event of the crucifixion of her Son took place. As far as we know, she was the only person to witness both the birth and the death of Jesus. Look again at Luke 2:25-35. What were Simeon's personal and prophetic words spoken to Mary in verse 35?

How do you see Simeon's prediction lived out in the scene at hand?

Suffering at the Cross

At the cross her station keeping
Stood the mournful mother weeping,
Close to Jesus to the last;

Through her heart, His sorrow sharing,
All His bitter anguish bearing,
Now at length the sword had passed.[32]

Nurturing a Heart of Humility

What an awesome band of faithful, humble followers of Jesus Christ we have just met! Indeed, they had nothing to gain by identifying with Jesus at the treacherous, tumultuous end of His life...and everything to lose! But those who followed faithfully were there at the best of times...and the worst of times...to the end. Rather than sidestep the life-threatening situation, they stayed at their station. Long before the familiar words "His faithful follower I would be, for by His hand He leadeth me"[33] were written, these followers were faithful.

Are you faithful, dear one, to follow the Lord, to feed on His Word (as we learned in our last lesson), to fellowship with His people, to further the needs of your family?

Lesson 24

Waiting on the Lord

Acts 1:12-14

ere we are! We made it! We are standing at the end of Mary's life as reported in the Bible. As we see Mary in today's lesson and mentally "rewind" to her beginnings, one thing is clear: Mary humbly accepted God's favor and maintained unwavering belief in God's promises. Hers is a picture of a woman of faith. As she said of herself while only a young woman, and as we've seen lived out in the intervening 33 years, "I am the Lord's servant" (Luke 1:38).[34]

From the Heart of God's Word...

As we say farewell to Mary here in the beginning of the book of Acts, we find her with a small band of believers.

1. First read Acts 1:1-3, a brief description of Jesus' ministry and of the 40 days the risen Lord was with the apostles. These were days spent in instruction regarding the kingdom of God.

2. Next read Acts 1:4-8. What instructions did Jesus give to those who believed in Him?

   —Remain (verse 4)

   —Wait (verses 4-5)

   —Receive (verse 8)

   —Witness (verse 8)

3. Now read Acts 1:9-11. Note the details given in each verse describing....

   ...the ascension (verse 9)—

   ...the appearing (verse 10)—

   ...the assurance (verse 11)—

4. Finally, read Acts 1:12-14. How did the faithful believers follow through on Jesus' instructions (verse 12)?

Where did they then go (verse 13)?

What did they do (verse 14)?

And who was also present with the eleven apostles (verse 14)?

From Your Heart...

- *Instructed Witnesses*—Jesus was faithful to give specific instruction to His faithful followers...including Mary. How did they respond to His instructions?

Now, how do you tend to respond to...

...instruction from the Bible?

...biblical teaching from others?

How does following instructions indicate a heart of humility?

- *Empowered Witnesses*—As one authority stated regarding verse 2, "This reference to the Holy Spirit sounds the chief theological note of The Acts—the work of the Holy Spirit."[35]

What is said about the Holy Spirit in...

...verse 5?

...verse 8?

Briefly, what teaching had Jesus already given to His disciples regarding the Holy Spirit in...

...John 14:16-17?

...John 14:26?

...John 15:26?

...John 16:8?

What further teaching does the New Testament give regarding the Holy Spirit in...

...1 Corinthians 3:16?

...1 Corinthians 6:19?

Can you recall a specific instance when the Holy Spirit empowered you to witness of Jesus Christ?

• *Praying Witnesses*—Jesus' followers prayed *while* they waited! How do you normally handle waiting? Do you fret and stew? Pace and worry? Or maybe I should ask, *do* you wait...or do you rush in without preparation, guidance, and instruction? Take a minute to think about (and note) how you generally deal with decision-making, dilemmas, and difficult tasks.

How does the humble obedience of these 120 people (Acts 1:15) encourage you to pray first and act later?

Nurturing a Heart of Humility

Most everyone would agree that there is quite a sentimental aura surrounding Mary, the mother of our Lord Jesus Christ. And there's no doubt that she was highly favored of the Lord (Luke 1:28-30). But in the end, where do we find Mary? Sitting for a portrait...or a statue? "On the road," sharing her story? Holding court? Doing interviews? Dictating her biography? Making a movie?

No, we find the humble Mary at prayer. (And no, she's not even leading the prayer meeting. She is simply praying along with the other pray-ers.) We find her waiting...just as her Son had instructed, waiting for the Holy Spirit.

*R*eady and willing, Thee to obey,
Silent, if need be, have Thine own way;
In full submission all do I give,
Nothing withhold, Lord, in me now live.[36]

Let's carry this image of Mary at prayer—this *real* image from Scripture—away with us in our hearts. May we take to heart Mary's many examples of humble service. May we as women after God's own heart follow in her humble footsteps as we journey through our lives as women, wives, mothers, fellow-sufferers, and servants in the church. And may we humbly wait on the Lord each and every day of our lives for His instructions. These practices will help you and me to nurture a heart of humility.

Lesson 25

Serving Through the Seasons

Summary

Truly, no woman has ever been as honored as Mary, the mother of our Lord Jesus Christ. Indeed, millions of people all over the world have named their daughters Mary. In fact, in the year 1975 at least 5,031,000 women in America alone bore the name of Mary or one of its variations.[37]

I'm sure you'll agree that Mary was a woman after God's own heart, a woman who exhibited the heart of a true servant. And, according to one source, "as a result, this humble peasant girl has been remembered and admired by millions throughout history."[38]

Let's remember now some of the seasons of Mary's life of service.

From the Heart of God's Word...

  Think through these aspects of Mary's life. Perhaps even take the time to turn through our previous lessons. Then share what impresses you about Mary's daily life and challenges at each season.

  1. *Mary, the teenager*—(Remember...scholars teach us that Mary was probably 12 to 14 years of age when we first meet her.)

  2. *Mary, the wife*—

  3. *Mary, the young mother of Jesus*—

  4. *Mary, the busy mother of many*—(As we've already learned, Mary had her hands full raising at least seven children!)

  5. *Mary, the homemaker*—(Mary's "occupation" is listed in *The Life Application Bible* as "homemaker."[39])

  6. *Mary, the widow*—(Tradition teaches that Mary tasted the bitter heartache of the loss of her husband, Joseph.)

7. *Mary, the sufferer*—(Mary also tasted the bitter heartache of the loss of a child, her Son, Jesus.)

8. *Mary, the worshiper*—(Mary and Joseph made sure they and their family followed God's commands regarding worship.)

9. *Mary, the pray-er*—(Our last glimpse of Mary is as a humble petitioner among many.)

From Your Heart...

- List at least ten marks of humility that you can recall from the life of Mary.

- Now note three things you can do (with the Lord's help) to nurture a heart of greater humility.

  —

  —

  —

When will you start, dear one? Pick a date, draw up a plan, and ask others to pray for you.

Nurturing a Heart of Humility

A Rare Commodity

Humility isn't a show we put on; in fact, if we think we're humble, we're probably not. And in our day of self-promotion, self-assertion, spotlighting "celebrities of the faith," and magnifying the flesh, this quality—so greatly valued by the Lord Jesus—is a rare commodity indeed....

A truly humble person looks for opportunities to give himself freely to others rather than holding back, to release rather than hoarding, to build up rather than tearing down, to serve rather than being served, to learn from others rather than clamoring for the teaching stand. How blessed are those who learn this early in life.[40]

Dear one, don't let another day pass! Take these treasured lessons from Mary's precious life...and look to the Lord for His help and enablement in nurturing a heart of genuine humility through all the seasons of life. As the Bible reminds us,

> ...all of you serve each other with humble spirits, for God gives special blessings to those who are humble, but sets himself against those who are proud. If you will humble yourselves under the mighty hand of God, in his good time he will lift you up (1 Peter 5:5-6 TLB).

*H*ow to Study the Bible —Some Practical Tips

By Jim George, Th.M.

One of the noblest pursuits a child of God can embark upon is to get to know and understand God better. The best way we can accomplish this is to look carefully at the book He has written, the Bible, which communicates who He is and His plan for mankind. There are a number of ways we can study the Bible, but one of the most effective and simple approaches to reading and understanding God's Word involves three simple steps:

Step 1: Observation—*What does the passage say?*

Step 2: Interpretation—*What does the passage mean?*

Step 3: Application—*What am I going to do about what the passage says and means?*

Observation is the first and most important step in the process. As you read the Bible text, you need to *look* carefully at what is said, and how it is said. Look for:

- *Terms, not words.* Words can have many meanings, but terms are words used in a specific way in a specific context. (For instance, the word *trunk* could apply to a tree, a car, or a storage box. However, when you read, "That tree has a very large trunk," you know exactly what the word means, which makes it a term.)

- *Structure.* If you look at your Bible, you will see that the text has units called *paragraphs* (indented or marked ¶). A paragraph is a complete unit of thought. You can discover the content of the author's message by noting and understanding each paragraph unit.

139

- *Emphasis.* The amount of space or the number of chapters or verses devoted to a specific topic will reveal the importance of that topic (for example, note the emphasis of Romans 9–11 and Psalm 119).

- *Repetition.* This is another way an author demonstrates that something is important. One reading of 1 Corinthians 13, where the author uses the word "love" nine times in only 13 verses, communicates to us that love is the focal point of these 13 verses.

- *Relationships between ideas.* Pay close attention, for example, to certain relationships that appear in the text:

  —Cause-and-effect: "Well done, good and faithful servant; you were faithful over a few things, I will make you ruler over many things" (Matthew 25:21).
  —Ifs and thens: "If My people who are called by My name will humble themselves, and pray and seek My face, and turn from their wicked ways, then I will hear from heaven and forgive their sin and heal their land" (2 Chronicles 7:14).
  —Questions and answers: "Who is the King of glory? The Lord strong and mighty" (Psalm 24:8).

- *Comparisons and contrasts.* For example, "You have heard that it was said...but I say to you..." (Matthew 5:21).

- *Literary form.* The Bible is literature, and the three main types of literature in the Bible are discourse (the epistles), prose (Old Testament history), and poetry (the Psalms). Considering the type of literature makes a great deal of difference when you read and interpret the Scriptures.

- *Atmosphere.* The author had a particular reason or burden for writing each passage, chapter, and book. Be sure you notice the mood or tone or urgency of the writing.

After you have considered these things, you then are ready to ask the "Wh" questions:

Who?	Who are the people in this passage?
What?	What is happening in this passage?
Where?	Where is this story taking place?
When?	What time (of day, of the year, in history) is it?

Asking these four "Wh" questions can help you notice terms and identify atmosphere. The answers will also enable you to use your imagination to recreate the scene you're reading about.

As you answer the "Wh" questions and imagine the event, you'll probably come up with some questions of your own. Asking those additional questions for understanding will help to build a bridge between observation (the first step) and interpretation (the second step) of the Bible study process.

Interpretation is discovering the meaning of a passage, the author's main thought or idea. Answering the questions that arise during observation will help you in the process of interpretation. Five clues (called "the five C's") can help you determine the author's main point(s):

- *Context.* You can answer 75 percent of your questions about a passage when you read the text. Reading the text involves looking at the near context (the verse immediately before and after) as well as the far context (the paragraph or the chapter that precedes and/or follows the passage you're studying).

- *Cross-references.* Let Scripture interpret Scripture. That is, let other passages in the Bible shed light on the passage you are looking at. At the same time, be careful not to assume that the same word or phrase in two different passages means the same thing.

- *Culture.* The Bible was written long ago, so when we interpret it, we need to understand it from the writers' cultural context.

- *Conclusion.* Having answered your questions for understanding by means of context, cross-reference, and culture, you can make a preliminary statement of the passage's meaning. Remember that if your passage consists of more than one paragraph, the author may be presenting more than one thought or idea.

- *Consultation.* Reading books known as commentaries, which are written by Bible scholars, can help you interpret Scripture.

Application is why we study the Bible. We want our lives to change; we want to be obedient to God and to grow more like Jesus Christ. After we have observed a passage and interpreted or understood it to the best of our ability, we must then apply its truth to our own life.

You'll want to ask the following questions of every passage of Scripture you study:

- How does the truth revealed here affect my relationship with God?
- How does this truth affect my relationship with others?
- How does this truth affect me?
- How does this truth affect my response to the enemy, Satan?

The application step is not completed by simply answering these questions; the key is *putting into practice* what God has taught you in your study. Although at any given moment you cannot be consciously applying *every*thing you're learning in Bible study, you can be consciously applying *some*thing. And when you work on applying a truth to your life, God will bless your efforts by, as noted earlier, conforming you to the image of Jesus Christ.

Helpful Bible Study Resources:

Concordance—Young's or Strong's

Bible dictionary—Unger's or Holman's

Webster's dictionary

The Zondervan Pictorial Encyclopedia of the Bible

Manners and Customs of the Bible,
    James M. Freeman

Books on Bible Study:

The Joy of Discovery, Oletta Wald

Enjoy Your Bible, Irving L. Jensen

How to Read the Bible for All It's Worth, Gordon
    Fee & Douglas Stuart

A Layman's Guide to Interpreting the Bible,
    W. Henrichsen

Living by the Book, Howard G. Hendricks

$\mathcal{L}$eading a Bible Study Discussion Group

$\mathcal{W}$hat a privilege it is to lead a Bible study! And what joy and excitement await you as you delve into the Word of God and help others to discover its life-changing truths. If God has called you to lead a Bible study group, I know you'll be spending much time in prayer and planning and giving much thought to being an effective leader. I also know that taking the time to read through the following tips will help you to navigate the challenges of leading a Bible study discussion group and enjoying the effort and opportunity.

The Leader's Roles

As a Bible study group leader, you'll find your role changing back and forth from *expert* to *cheerleader* to *lover* to *referee* during the course of a session.

Since you're the leader, group members will look to you to be the *expert* guiding them through the material. So be well prepared. In fact, be over-prepared so that you know the material better than any group member does. Start your study early in the week and let its message simmer all week long. (You might even work several lessons ahead so that you have in mind the big picture and the overall direction of the study.) Be ready to share some additional gems that your group members wouldn't have discovered on their own. That extra insight from your study time—or that comment from a wise Bible teacher or scholar, that clever saying, that keen observation from another believer, and even an appropriate joke—adds an element of fun and keeps Bible study from becoming routine, monotonous, and dry.

Next, be ready to be the group's *cheerleader.* Your energy and enthusiasm for the task at hand can be contagious. It can also stimulate people to get more involved in their personal study as well as in the group discussion.

Third, be the *lover,* the one who shows a genuine concern for the members of the group. You're the one who will establish the atmosphere of the group. If you laugh and have fun, the group members will laugh and have fun. If you hug, they will hug. If you care, they will care. If you share, they will share. If you love, they will love. So pray every day to love the women God has placed in your group. Ask Him to show you how to love them with His love.

Finally, as the leader, you'll need to be the *referee* on occasion. That means making sure everyone has an equal opportunity to speak. That's easier to do when you operate under the assumption that every member of the group has something worthwhile to contribute. So, trusting that the Lord has taught each person during the week, act on that assumption.

Expert, cheerleader, lover, and referee—these four roles of the leader may make the task seem overwhelming. But that's not bad if it keeps you on your knees praying for your group.

A Good Start

Beginning on time, greeting people warmly, and opening in prayer gets the study off to a good start. Know what you want to have happen during your time together and make sure those things get done. That kind of order means comfort for those involved.

Establish a format and let the group members know what that format is. People appreciate being in a Bible study that focuses on the Bible. So keep the discussion on the topic and move the group through the questions. Tangents are often hard to avoid—and even harder to rein in. So be sure to focus on the answers to questions about the specific passage at hand. After all, the purpose of the group is Bible study!

Finally, as someone has accurately observed, "Personal growth is one of the by-products of any effective small group. This growth is achieved when people are recognized and accepted by others. The more friendliness, mutual trust, respect, and warmth exhibited, the more likely that the member will find pleasure in the group, and, too, the more likely she will work hard toward the accomplishment of the group's goals. The effective leader will strive to reinforce desirable traits" (source unknown).

A Dozen Helpful Tips

Here is a list of helpful suggestions for leading a Bible study discussion group:

1. Arrive early, ready to focus fully on others and give of yourself. If you have to do any last-minute preparation, review, re-grouping, or praying, do it in the car. Don't dash in, breathless, harried, late, still tweaking your plans.

2. Check out your meeting place in advance. Do you have everything you need—tables, enough chairs, a black-board, hymnals if you plan to sing, coffee, etc.?

3. Greet each person warmly by name as she arrives. After all, you've been praying for these women all week long, so let each VIP know that you're glad she's arrived.

4. Use name tags for at least the first two or three weeks.

5. Start on time no matter what—even if only one person is there!

6. Develop a pleasant but firm opening statement. You might say, "This lesson was great! Let's get started so we can enjoy all of it!" or "Let's pray before we begin our lesson."

7. Read the questions, but don't hesitate to reword them on occasion. Rather than reading an entire paragraph of instructions, for instance, you might say, "Question 1 asks us to list some ways that Christ displayed humility. Lisa, please share one way Christ displayed humility."

8. Summarize or paraphrase the answers given. Doing so will keep the discussion focused on the topic; eliminate digressions; help avoid or clear up any misunderstandings of the text; and keep each group member aware of what the others are saying.

9. Keep moving and don't add any of your own questions to the discussion time. It's important to get through the study guide questions. So if a cut-and-dried answer is called for, you don't need to comment with anything other than a "thank you." But when the question asks for an opinion or an application (for instance, "How can this truth help us in our marriages?" or "How do *you* find time for your quiet time?"), let all who want to contribute.

10. Affirm each person who contributes, especially if the contribution was very personal, painful to share, or a quiet person's rare statement. Make everyone who shares a hero by saying something like "Thank you for sharing that insight from your own life," or "We certainly appreciate what God has taught you. Thank you for letting us in on it."

11. Watch your watch, put a clock right in front of you, or consider using a timer. Pace the discussion so that you meet your cut-off time, especially if you want time to pray. Stop at the designated time even if you haven't finished the lesson. Remember that everyone has worked through the study once; you are simply going over it again.

12. End on time. You can only make friends with your group members by ending on time or even a little early! Besides,

members of your group have the next item on their agenda to attend to—picking up children from the nursery, babysitter, or school; heading home to tend to matters there; running errands; getting to bed; or spending some time with their husbands. So let them out *on time!*

Five Common Problems

In any group, you can anticipate certain problems. Here are some common ones that can arise, along with helpful solutions:

1. *The incomplete lesson*—Right from the start, establish the policy that if someone has not done the lesson, it is best for her not to answer the questions. But do try to include her responses to questions that ask for opinions or experiences. Everyone can share some thoughts in reply to a question like, "Reflect on what you know about both athletic and spiritual training and then share what you consider to be the essential elements of training oneself in godliness."

2. *The gossip*—The Bible clearly states that gossiping is wrong, so you don't want to allow it in your group. Set a high and strict standard by saying, "I am not comfortable with this conversation," or "We [not *you*] are gossiping, ladies. Let's move on."

3. *The talkative member*—Here are three scenarios and some possible solutions for each.

   a. The problem talker may be talking because she has done her homework and is excited about something she has to share. She may also know more about the subject than the others and, if you cut her off, the rest of the group may suffer.

SOLUTION: Respond with a comment like: "Sarah, you are making very valuable contributions. Let's see if we can get some reactions from the others," or "I know Sarah can answer this. She's really done her homework. How about some of the rest of you?"

b. The talkative member may be talking because she has *not* done her homework and wants to contribute, but she has no boundaries.

SOLUTION: Establish at the first meeting that those who have not done the lesson do not contribute except on opinion or application questions. You may need to repeat this guideline at the beginning of each session.

c. The talkative member may want to be heard whether or not she has anything worthwhile to contribute.

SOLUTION: After subtle reminders, be more direct, saying, "Betty, I know you would like to share your ideas, but let's give others a chance. I'll call on you later."

4. *The quiet member*—Here are two scenarios and possible solutions.

a. The quiet member wants the floor but somehow can't get the chance to share.

SOLUTION: Clear the path for the quiet member by first watching for clues that she wants to speak (moving to the edge of her seat, looking as if she wants to speak, perhaps even starting to say something) and then saying, "Just a second. I think Chris wants to say something." Then, of course, make her a hero!

b. The quiet member simply doesn't want the floor.

SOLUTION: "Chris, what answer do you have on question 2?" or "Chris, what do you think about...?" Usually after a shy person has contributed a few times, she will become more confident and more ready to share. Your role is to provide an opportunity where there is *no* risk of a wrong answer. But occasionally a group member will tell you that she would rather not be called on. Honor her request, but from time to time ask her privately if she feels ready to contribute to the group discussions.

In fact, give all your group members the right to pass. During your first meeting, explain that any time a group member does not care to share an answer, she may simply say, "I pass." You'll want to repeat this policy at the beginning of every group session.

5. *The wrong answer*—Never tell a group member that she has given a wrong answer, but at the same time never let a wrong answer go by.

SOLUTION: Either ask if someone else has a different answer or ask additional questions that will cause the right answer to emerge. As the women get closer to the right answer, say, "We're getting warmer! Keep thinking! We're almost there!"

Learning from Experience

Immediately after each Bible study session, evaluate the group discussion time using this checklist. You may also want a member of your group (or an assistant or trainee or outside observer) to evaluate you periodically.

May God strengthen—and encourage!—you as you assist others in the discovery of His many wonderful truths.

Notes

1. Taken from Elizabeth George, *A Woman After God's Own Heart*® (Eugene, OR: Harvest House Publishers, 1997), pp. 24-29.

2. Elizabeth George, *Loving God with All Your Mind* (Eugene, OR: Harvest House Publishers, 1994).

3. M. R. DeHaan and Henry G. Bosch, *Our Daily Bread* (Grand Rapids, MI: Zondervan Publishing House, 1982), November 3.

4. Herbert Lockyer, *All the Women of the Bible* (Grand Rapids, MI: Zondervan Publishing House, 1975), p. 50.

5. Frank S. Mead, *12,000 Religious Quotations*, quoting Harry Ward Beecher (Grand Rapids, MI: Baker Book House, 1989), p. 267.

6. Paul N. Benware, *Luke, The Gospel of the Son of Man* (Chicago: Moody Press, 1985), p. 29.

7. Charles R. Swindoll, *Wisdom for the Way* (Nashville: J. Countryman, 2001), p. 396.

8. J. Oswald Sanders, as cited by Charles R. Swindall, *The Tale of the Tardy Oxcart* (Nashville: Word Publishing, 1998), p. 279.

9. Roy B. Zuck, *The Speaker's Quote Book*, quoting Bernard of Clairvaux (Grand Rapids, MI: Kregel Publications, 1997), p. 203.

10. Gien Karssen, *Her Name Is Woman* (Colorado Springs: NavPress, 1975), p. 131.

11. *Life Application Bible Commentary—Luke* (Wheaton, IL: Tyndale House Publishers, Inc., 1997), p. 41.

12. Benware, *Luke, The Gospel of the Son of Man,* p. 35.

13. D. L. Moody, *Notes from My Bible and Thoughts from My Library* (Grand Rapids, MI: Baker Book House, 1979), p. 119.

14. Zuck, *The Speaker's Quote Book,* quoting Vance Havner, p. 268.

15. Merrill F. Unger, *Unger's Bible Dictionary* (Chicago: Moody Press, 1980), p. 890.

16. John F. MacArthur, *The MacArthur New Testament Commentary—Matthew 1-7* (Chicago: Moody Press, 1985), p. 28.

17. *Life Application Bible Commentary—Matthew* (Wheaton, IL: Tyndale House Publishers, Inc., 1996), p. 25.

18. Ibid., p. 30.

19. Benware, *Luke, The Gospel of the Son of Man,* p. 36.

20. Ibid., p. 37.

21. Robert Jamieson, A. R. Fausset, and David Brown, *Commentary on the Whole Bible* (Grand Rapids, MI: Zondervan Publishing House, 1973), p. 994.

22. Zuck, *The Speaker's Quotebook,* quoting Andrew Murray, p. 203.

23. William Hendricksen, *Exposition of the Gospel According to Luke* (Grand Rapids, MI: Baker Book House, 1978), p. 185.

24. Zuck, *The Speaker's Quotebook,* quoting Andrew Murray, p. 204.

25. Ibid., quoting *The Reader's Digest,* p. 263.

26. *Life Application Bible Commentary—Luke,* p. 207.

27. John Oxenham.

28. G. Coleman Luck, *Luke, the Gospel of the Son of Man,* quoting J. C. Ryle (Chicago: Moody Press, 1970), p. 88.

29. Benware, *Luke, the Gospel of the Son of Man,* p. 94.

30. *God's Treasury of Virtues,* quoting John M. Drescher (Tulsa, OK: Honor Books, 1995), p. 297.

31. Jamieson, Fausset, and Brown, *Commentary on the Whole Bible,* p. 1073.

32. Hendricksen, *Exposition of the Gospel According to Luke,* p. 171.

33. William Bradbury and Joseph Gilmore, "He Leadeth Me."

34. Sid Buzzell, general editor, *The Leadership Bible* (Grand Rapids, MI: Zondervan Publishing House, 1998), p. 1195.

35. Charles F. Pfeiffer and Everett F. Harrison, *The Wycliffe Bible Commentary* (Chicago: Moody Press, 1973), p. 1125.

36. DeHaan and Bosch, *Our Daily Bread,* quoting C. F. Warren, September 20.

37. Lockyer, *All the Women of the Bible,* p. 92.

38. Buzzell, *The Leadership Bible,* p. 1195.

39. *The Life Application Bible* (Wheaton, IL: Tyndale House Publishers, Inc., 1988), p. 1471.

40. Swindoll, *Wisdom for the Way,* p. 150.

Bibliography

Benware, Paul N. *Luke, The Gospel of the Son of Man.* Chicago: Moody Press, 1985.

Hendricksen, William. *Exposition of the Gospel According to Luke.* Grand Rapids, MI: Baker Book House, 1978.

Jamieson, Robert, A. R. Fausset, and David Brown. *Commentary on the Whole Bible.* Grand Rapids, MI: Zondervan Publishing House, 1973.

Life Application Bible Commentary—Luke. Wheaton, IL: Tyndale House Publishers, Inc., 1997.

Life Application Bible Commentary—Matthew. Wheaton, IL: Tyndale House Publishers, Inc., 1996.

Luck, G. Coleman. *Luke, the Gospel of the Son of Man.* Chicago: Moody Press, 1970.

MacArthur, John F. *The MacArthur Study Bible.* Nashville: Word Publishing, 1997.

_____. *The MacArthur New Testament Commentary— Matthew 1–7.* Chicago: Moody Press, 1985.

Morris, Leon. *Tyndale New Testament Commentaries—The Gospel According to St. Luke.* Grand Rapids, MI: William B. Eerdmans Publishing Company, 1976.

Pfeiffer, Charles F., and Everett F. Harrison. *The Wycliffe Bible Commentary.* Chicago: Moody Press, 1973.

Tasker, R. B. G. *The Tyndale New Testament Commentaries—The Gospel According to St. John.* Grand Rapids, MI: William B. Eerdmans Publishing Company, 1976.

Thomas, Robert L., and Stanley N. Gundry. *A Harmony of the Gospels.* Chicago: Moody Press, 1981.

Personal Notes

A Woman After God's Own Heart® Study Series

BIBLE STUDIES FOR BUSY WOMEN

"God wrote the Bible to change hearts and lives. Every study in this series is written with that in mind—and is specially focused on helping Christian women know how God desires for them to live."
—Elizabeth George

Sharing wisdom gleaned from more than 20 years as a women's Bible study teacher, Elizabeth has prepared insightful lessons that can be completed in 15 to 20 minutes per day. Each lesson includes thought-provoking questions and insights, Bible study tips, instructions for leading a discussion group, and a "heart response" section to make the Bible passage more personal.

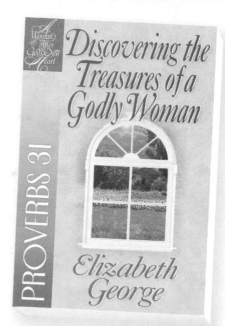

Proverbs 31 0-7369-0818-8

Philippians 0-7369-0289-9

1 Peter 0-7369-0290-2

1 Timothy 0-7369-0665-7

Judges/Ruth 0-7369-0498-0

Esther 0-7369-0489-1

James 0-7369-0490-5

Life of Mary 0-7369-0300-3

Life of Sarah 0-7369-0301-1

About the Author

Elizabeth George is a bestselling author and speaker whose passion is to teach the Bible in a way that changes women's lives. For information about Elizabeth's books or speaking ministry, to sign up for her mailings, or to share how God has used this book in your life, please write to Elizabeth at:

Elizabeth George
P.O. Box 2879
Belfair, WA 98528

Toll free fax/phone: 1-800-542-4611
www.ElizabethGeorge.com

Books by Elizabeth George

- Beautiful in God's Eyes
- Encouraging Words for a Woman After God's Own Heart®
- God's Wisdom for a Woman's Life
- Life Management for Busy Women
- Loving God with All Your Mind
- A Mom After God's Own Heart
- Powerful Promises for Every Woman
- The Remarkable Women of the Bible
- A Wife After God's Own Heart
- A Woman After God's Own Heart®
- A Woman After God's Own Heart® Deluxe Edition
- A Woman After God's Own Heart® Prayer Journal
- A Woman's Call to Prayer
- A Woman's High Calling
- A Woman's Walk with God
- A Young Woman After God's Own Heart
- A Young Woman's Call to Prayer

Children's Books

- God's Wisdom for Little Girls

Study Guides

- Beautiful in God's Eyes Growth & Study Guide
- God's Wisdom for a Woman's Life Growth & Study Guide
- Life Management for Busy Women Growth & Study Guide
- Loving God with All Your Mind Growth & Study Guide
- A Mom After God's Own Heart Growth & Study Guide
- Powerful Promises for Every Woman Growth & Study Guide
- The Remarkable Women of the Bible Growth & Study Guide
- A Wife After God's Own Heart Growth & Study Guide
- A Woman After God's Own Heart® Growth & Study Guide
- A Woman's Call to Prayer Growth & Study Guide
- A Woman's High Calling Growth & Study Guide
- A Woman's Walk with God Growth & Study Guide

Books by Jim & Elizabeth George

- God Loves His Precious Children
- God's Wisdom for Little Boys
- Powerful Promises for Every Couple
- Powerful Promises for Every Couple Growth & Study Guide

Books by Jim George

- God's Man of Influence
- A Husband After God's Own Heart
- A Man After God's Own Heart
- Remarkable Prayers of the Bible
- A Young Man After God's Own Heart